CLIENT PRAISE

Highly recommend Miss Sylvia!

I have had many readings over the years with Miss Sylvia and I am completely blown away by her accuracy. She is the best Lenormand card reader I've ever had. Thank you for being a great listener and for giving me peace of mind.

Client Paul K.
July 2017

Very gifted and wise person!

Sylvia's readings were very detailed and insightful. Her interpretations were explained in understandable ways. I am so grateful Miss Sylvia was able to help me to make a difficult choice.

Liane
November 2019

Just what I needed!

I just wanted to say thank you for all your readings. I can't tell you how much it has helped me. All of your predictions became true. But most important you gave me peace of mind and guidance.
Thank you again!
 Sincerely,
Jake

October 2022

Miss Sylvia gave me absolutely fantastic readings!

I've now had 5 and all of them been spot on. Her predictions played out as she described. I highly recommend her as a Lenormand card reader.
  -Rachel-
July 2018

Great reader and teacher!

I met Miss Sylvia through her mother. After her mother's death, I continued to consult Miss Sylvia for readings. She always gave me accurate and helpful readings. After a while, I got so fascinated about the Lenormand cards that I wanted to learn how to read them myself. Miss Sylvia taught me the traditional Lenormand system and I am so grateful I found her. She is very patient and incredibly talented.
I highly recommend Miss Sylvia as a Lenormand card reader and teacher.

Samantha K.
February 2020

THE LENORMAND
LEARNING THE SKILL TO TRANSLATE THE LENORMAND LANGUAGE

SYLVIA KA'UHANE

Copyright © 2024 by Sylvia Ka'Uhane

All rights reserved.

No portion of this book may be reproduced in any form without written permission from the publisher or author, except as permitted by U.S. copyright law.

ACKNOWLEDGMENTS

I want to acknowledge a few people who are very important in my life:

This book is for my mother, Wieslawa; a thank you that she was always there for me. I am very grateful I had her in my life. I will love you forever. Also, I'd like to thank my true friends and advisors, who are like parents to me, and Carlos and Trisha for always being there for me. To Luis, who brightened up my life after my mother's death, and thank you to my friend Derek, whose writing always inspired me and helped me get going with this book. Thank you to Alicja, who taught me, "Done is better than perfect!" Special thanks to my lifelong true friends Dennis, Kitana, Heike, Barbara, Gregor, Norbert, and Christine - who I can always count on and who encourage and believe in me. I love you guys! I also want to say thank you to my editor, Dawn Heimer, for guiding me through the whole process of publishing my book and helping me share my knowledge and passion for the Lenormand.

I want to give thanks to all the people who came to me and let me read the stories of their lives, who trusted me and shared my passion for the Lenormand.

Thank you!

CONTENTS

1. INTRODUCTION — 1
2. WHAT IS LENORMAND? — 2
3. HOW TO ASK A QUESTION AND WHAT TO ASK — 3
4. HOW TO CHARGE A CARD — 5
5. CARD #1 - THE RIDER - 9 OF HEARTS — 9
6. CARD #2 - CLOVER - 6 OF DIAMONDS — 14
7. CARD #3 - SHIP - 10 OF SPADES — 18
8. CARD #4 - HOUSE - KING OF HEARTS — 23
9. CARD #5 - TREE - 7 OF HEARTS — 27
10. CARD #6 - CLOUDS - KING OF CLUBS — 34
11. CARD #7 - SNAKE - QUEEN OF CLUBS — 40
12. CARD #8 - COFFIN - 9 OF DIAMONDS — 46
13. CARD #9 - BOUQUET - QUEEN OF SPADES — 53
14. CARD #10 - SCYTHE - JACK OF DIAMONDS — 58
15. CARD #11 - WHIP - JACK OF CLUBS — 64
16. CARD #12 - BIRDS - 7 OF DIAMONDS — 71
17. CARD #13 - CHILD - JACK OF SPADES — 77
18. CARD #14 - FOX - NINE OF CLUBS — 83
19. CARD #15 - BEAR - 10 OF CLUBS — 88
20. CARD #16 - STARS - 6 OF HEARTS — 93

21.	CARD #17 - STORK - QUEEN OF HEARTS	99
22.	CARD #18 - DOG - 10 OF HEARTS	105
23.	CARD #19 - TOWER - 6 OF SPADES	110
24.	CARD #20 - GARDEN - 8 OF SPADES	117
25.	CARD #21 - MOUNTAIN - 8 OF CLUBS	123
26.	CARD #22 - CROSSROADS - QUEEN OF DIAMONDS	130
27.	CARD #23 - MICE - 7 OF CLUBS	137
28.	CARD #24 - HEART - JACK OF HEARTS	144
29.	CARD #25 - RING - ACE OF CLUBS	151
30.	CARD #26 - BOOK - 10 OF DIAMONDS	157
31.	CARD #27 - LETTER - 7 OF SPADES	164
32.	CARD #28 AND #29 - MAN - ACE OF HEARTS & WOMAN - ACE OF SPADES	170
33.	CARD #30 - LILIES - KING OF SPADES	177
34.	CARD #31 - SUN - ACE OF DIAMONDS	187
35.	CARD #32 - MOON - 8 OF HEARTS	193
36.	CARD #33 - KEY - 8 OF DIAMONDS	200
37.	CARD #34 - FISH - KING OF DIAMONDS	206
38.	CARD #35 - ANCHOR - 9 OF SPADES	212
39.	CARD #36 - CROSS - 6 OF CLUBS	218
40.	HOW TO ASK A YES/NO QUESTION	225
41.	THE LINE READING	227
42.	THE BOX SPREAD	229
43.	TIPS ON HOW TO READ A GRAND TABLEAU	236
44.	A REAL READING USING THE GRAND TABLEAU	250
45.	CLEARING THE CARDS	262
46.	CONCLUSION	263

Chapter One
Introduction

This is a practical guide on how to understand and read the Lenormand cards. In the beginning, it will take a little time and practice to know how to translate the Lenormand language, but once you master this, Lenormand will become your best friend! A friend you can ask any question to, and you will get a straightforward, honest answer. In this book, you will find readings I performed for my clients and their feedback on how my predictions played out. I have changed the names of my clients to protect their privacy, and they gave me permission to write about their stories.

Now, I would like to introduce myself! I am Sylvia Ka'uhane, a professional Lenormand card reader from Hamburg, Germany. As a child, my beloved mother introduced me to the traditional Petit Lenormand system. In my childhood, I saw it as a game, and I loved listening to my mom's readings and predictions. It was like stories that became true. Cartomancy has always excited me, and I love helping people choose the right path, have peace of mind, and ease their stresses and worries with my card readings. In September 2019, my mother passed away, and I continued her card-reading tradition to honor her. After her death, my Lenormand reading skills drastically improved as if she were giving me insights. I know she's always around and guides my readings. Energy never dies...it just transforms into a different form.

Chapter Two
What is Lenormand?

Lenormand is a 200-year-old divination tool from Europe. It consists of 36 cards and is a very popular tool used in cartomancy, especially in Germany and France. The deck is named by Mademoiselle Marie Anne Adelaide Lenormand (1772-1843). She was a very famous French fortune teller during the Napoleonic era. She is considered the greatest cartomancer of all time, but Mademoiselle Lenormand did not create this deck or the system. It was only named by her for selling purposes. Despite this, Mademoiselle Lenormand is an inspiration for many card readers.

The Grand Tableau, French for "Large Table," uses all 36 cards of the Lenormand deck, laying them out in a grid. This spread provides a detailed and nuanced view of someone's past and present, covering relationships, careers, finances, and personal well-being. It gives you a snapshot of someone's life at a glance, with the relationships between the cards revealing complex interactions and influences. Each position in the Grand Tableau is considered a "house" that influences the meaning of the card in that position. The first card is in the house of Rider (Card 1), the second in the house of Clover (Card 2), and so on.

Regarding which Lenormand deck to choose, I recommend the Rana George Lenormand cards. Her deck includes four additional cards beyond the traditional 36 cards: Spirit (#37), Incense Burner (#38), Bed (#39), and Market (#40). Using the Rana George "frees up" some of the traditional cards to provide broader interpretations, as I will describe in the examples.

Chapter Three

How to Ask a Question and What to Ask

Asking a clear question can get you a clear answer.

The question or the context is everything! It is just so massively important because Lenormand is lexical. The cards respond directly to the question that you ask. The more specific the question, the more specific the answer is. Let's formulate a specific question!

Examples:

- What may I experience today?
- How will my day go?
- Will my meeting with my boss end positive?
- Am I going to receive the refund I asked for?
- How will my trip go?
- Is John being honest with me?
- Will I be able to retire this year?
- Am I passing this final exam?
- Is John being faithful?

There is no limit. You can ask the Lenormand everything! Now, while you are shuffling the cards, focus only on ONE specific question, and please don't think about other things like work, an argument, or a TV show. You should quiet your mind and meditate before asking the cards. This is very important because the cards are absorbing the energy that's going on in your mind. I don't recommend doing the cards when one is stressed out or anxious because the cards will reflect that anxiety.

Chapter Four
How to Charge a Card

Charging a card in the Lenormand deck (or in any divinatory system) is a process meant to infuse the card with a specific intention, energy, or focus. This practice can enhance readings by directing attention and intention more specifically. Here's a general guide on how to charge a card in the Lenormand deck:

Select Your Card

Choose the card you wish to charge. This could be based on a specific question, area of life, or the focus of your reading. In Lenormand readings, the significator card (often the Man or Woman card representing the querent) is commonly charged, but any card can be charged depending on your intention.

Clear Your Space

Start by clearing your space and your deck of any previous energies. You can do this through smudging with sage, palo santo, or using incense. Some prefer to use sound cleansing with bells or singing bowls. Ensure your space feels clean and conducive to focus and intention.

Focus Your Intention

Take a few moments to focus on your intention for the reading or the specific question you are seeking insight into. Clearly articulate this intention in your mind or out loud. Your intention should be direct, clear, and focused.

Hold the Card

Hold the card you are charging between your hands. Some prefer to place it over their heart or forehead (third eye area) to connect more deeply with the card's energy.

Visualize and Channel Energy

Close your eyes and visualize your intention flowing from you into the card. You can imagine this as a light, energy, or even a specific color that represents your intention. Feel the energy moving from your body, through your hands, and into the card. Take as long as you need for this step, ensuring the card is fully imbued with your intention.

Verbalize Your Intention (Optional)

While holding the card, you may also choose to verbalize your intention, saying something like, "I charge this card with the intention of revealing insights into [specific question or area of focus]." This can help solidify your intention and enhance the charging process.

Conclude with Gratitude

Once you feel the card has been sufficiently charged, conclude the process by expressing gratitude to the card, your guides, or the universe for the insights and guidance provided. This helps to seal the energy and reinforces the connection between you and the card.

Use the Card in Your Reading

Place the charged card back into your deck, shuffle, and proceed with your reading as usual, keeping your focus on the intention you've set.

Reflect

After the reading, take some time to reflect on the insights provided and how the charged card influenced the guidance received. This can help you understand the effectiveness of your charging process and refine it for future readings.

THE LENORMAND

Charging cards can be a deeply personal and intuitive process, so feel free to adapt these steps to suit your preferences and beliefs. The key is to maintain a clear focus on your intention and to connect with the card in a meaningful way.

Next, let's take a close look at each of the 36 Lenormand cards and how to read them when it comes to relationships, describing a person, health, money, advice, an object, timing, and understanding a Grand Tableau. I have **bolded the text** in certain places either for emphasis or to highlight the primary features of a card.

I will explain the near/far method, which interprets the outcomes by comparing the distance of the cards from the Significator. When I describe every single card, I talk about being **very close** to and **close** to the Significator and **far** from and **very far** from the Significator.

S = Significator

The cards that are very close to the Significator are touching the Man/Woman card. The cards that are close to the Significator are touching the very close cards. The cards that are far from the Significator are touching the close cards. The very far cards are touching the far cards. Here is an example:

- The A cards are the very close cards; they are touching the Significator directly.

- The B cards are the ones that are close; they are touching the very close cards.

- The C cards are the far cards; they are touching the close cards.

- The D cards are the very far cards; they are touching the far cards.

Chapter Five

Card #1 - The Rider - 9 of Hearts

The message sent is not always the message received.

- Virginia Satir -

The Rider #1 is a **neutral** card because it is highly influenced by the surrounding cards. Negative cards around the Rider bring bad news, and positive cards around the Rider bring good news.

- The core meaning of the Rider is **NEWS**

- The Rider card is all about movement and arrival

- News will be coming your way, either by mail, email, text, a call, or any kind of message/information

- It could also be a **visitor** arriving

- An unexpected visitor

- A delivery

- Something new

- A messenger

- Movement ahead

IN A RELATIONSHIP:

- In a relationship, reading for a single person, the Rider could be a new relationship, especially if you get the Rider + Heart combination.

- Depending on the question, if you get the Rider as the last card in a line reading, it stands for leaving/going away.

    - For example, my client Lisa asked me after she broke up with her boyfriend, "Will he come back to me?" I pulled Letter + Garden + Rider. This combination means Lisa will hear from him, but he will not come back to her.

- A new friendship

- A flirt

DESCRIBING A PERSON:

- When I want the cards to describe a person, and the rider comes up, I know it's a very fit person. He or she may be active with an outgoing personality.

- Athletic looking
- Strong legs
- Confident
- Well dressed
- It can stand for a delivery person (mailman)

HEALTH AND BODY PART:

- Anatomically, the Rider represents the legs, feet, ankles, knees, and joints.
  - For example, a friend of mine experienced knee pain and wanted to know what advice the cards would give. I pulled Rider + Coffin. This means she should rest!

MONEY:

- In a money reading, the Rider brings news about something coming. This could be good or bad; it all depends on the cards around the Rider. As we discussed earlier, the Rider is a neutral card that is highly influenced by the surrounding cards.
- Can be a check or a bill coming in

ADVICE:

- In an advice reading, the Rider says, "Keep moving forward!"
- Move on from this situation

OBJECT:

- As an object, the Rider can represent a bicycle, motorcycle, or horse

TIMIMG:

- When I ask about timing and the Rider shows up, that means it will happen very fast. The Rider is about speed and swiftness.

- One day

- January

IN A GRAND TABLEAU, If the Rider is very close or close to the Significator card, it means that news is on its way. What kind of news depends on the cards around the Rider. When surrounded by negative cards, the news will be negative. When surrounded by positive cards, the news will be positive. I always look in which direction the Rider is heading. In other words, which card comes after the rider?

For example, Rider + Clouds = Troubling news, and Rider + Sun = Positive news

The news might be coming from a foreign country if the Rider is far or very far from the Man/Woman card.

Card Combination Examples:

- Rider + Tree = Health-related information

- Rider + Bear = Finance related information

- Rider + Cross = Troublesome information

- Rider + Tower = Official news

- Rider + Lily = News from a family member

Whenever I have Rider + House in a daily draw, I know somebody is coming to visit me that day. A similar combination is Rider + The Bed Card #39 (from the Rana George Lenormand deck). Rider + Bed could mean that a lover is coming to visit.

Client Example:

After her interview, my client Nancy asked me: "Should I accept this offer?" I pulled:

Ring + Rider + Crossroads

My answer: No, walk away from the offer and choose a different path.

Interpretation:

Lenormand spreads are read in pairs like a sentence. We read from left to right. The Rider is heading away from the Ring towards the Crossroads. Also, I use DIRECTIONAL READING - I look where the Rider is heading towards.

DIRECTIONAL READING means interpreting the cards based on the direction the figure or symbol within the cards are facing or pointing towards and suggests whether a person is moving towards or away from something, the focus of attention, or where a client should direct efforts for the best results.

Here is another example of DIRECTIONAL READING:

Stork + Mountain

In this combination, the Stork is flying towards the mountain. In other words, the Stork is going towards obstacles and delays, or progress is blocked. Now, if we get the Mountain + Stork, that tells us that the Stork is overcoming the obstacles and delays - the Stork is flying away from the mountain.

In the Rana George deck, the Stork is flying from left to right, so when doing directional readings, it is easier to see and understand where the Stork is heading and what it is moving towards. If you have a Lenormand card deck where the Stork is flying from right to left, please remember we read the cards from LEFT TO RIGHT like reading a book.

The same applies to the Rider and Ship cards. We want to see where the Rider and the Ship are heading.

Chapter Six

Card #2 - Clover - 6 of Diamonds

I say luck is when an opportunity comes along, and you're prepared for it.
- Denzel Washington -

The Clover card #2 is a **positive** card.

- The core meaning of the Clover is **joy** and **good fortune**

- It symbolizes small **luck**, a chance/**opportunity**, good fortune, or a positive surprise

- It brings unexpected happiness and success

- It diminishes the negative vibe and sorrow of negative cards, especially if it lands on the right side of a negative card or if it lands at the end of a line reading

- If the Clover card lands on the right side of a negative card, it predicts the end of sorrow or the troubles will be of short duration

- If negative cards like Clouds, Coffin, Snake, Mice, and Scythe are on the right side of the Clover card, deceit and dilemmas from the past may return

IN A RELATIONSHIP:

- When I do a relationship reading, and the clover comes up, it talks about a reconciliation, a Quickie, a second chance, something unexpected positive, a new opportunity, or a happy relationship
  - For example, Coffin + Clover = reconciliation

- Also, in the context of love, the Clover can mean you are on someone's mind! Especially if the Book card is close, it indicates somebody has a crush on you or is thinking about you deeply.

DESCRIBING A PERSON:

- A person is lucky and has a positive and bubbly personality. It might also be a person who is unafraid of taking risks and chances.

- Passionate

- An uplifting personality

- Green eyes

HEALTH AND BODY PART:

- Anatomically speaking, the Clover represents the throat, esophagus, and lymphatic system. This is important to know for health readings.

- Homeopathy

- If asking for an outcome of a disease, the Clover predicts recovery

- Also, the Clover represents greens, vegetables, and homeopath

MONEY:

- In a money reading, the Clover is a sign that the financial situation will improve a little. Every time I do a money reading, and the Clover shows up, it means unexpected money is coming in. It may not be a big amount, but money is coming in!

ADVICE:

- In an advice reading, the Clover card says to stay positive and grab that opportunity as long as it's there. Remember, the Clover is short-lived!

- Take a chance!

OBJECTS:

- As an object, the Clover could represent a lottery ticket, a lucky charm, green vegetables, and grass

TIMING:

- When I ask the cards about timing, and the Clover shows up, it means a couple of days, 2 days, 2 weeks, or a short time

- February

IN A GRAND TABLEAU:

If the Clover is very close or close to the Significator (Man/Woman card) card, it indicates luck. For example, in opportunities and progress, unless it's surrounded by negative cards like the Clouds or Cross, then there will be sorrows but fortunately of short duration.

If the Clover card is far or very far from the Significator, then it talks about disappointments and dissatisfaction for the Significator. The opportunities are out of reach for the duration of the spread. If the Clover is far away from the Man/Woman card and surrounded by challenging, negative cards, this indicates hidden despair and quiet suffering.

If the Clover card lands in the house of the Clouds, that means the problems and troubles will clear up!

Chapter Seven
Card #3 - Ship - 10 of Spades

*Life is a journey;
it's not where you end up,
but it's how you got there.
- Unknown -*

The Ship card #3 is a **neutral** card because it is influenced by the surrounding cards. It's the only card with an engine!

- The core meaning of the Ship is **successful commerce** and **movement**

- It symbolizes **travel**, vacation, distance, **a change**, a transition, a **move**, a relocation, a transfer. It shows where the energy is flowing, and it also talks about moving away/leaving.

- In the traditional meaning of the Ship, it could also be an inheritance, especially if the Ship is next to the Coffin
    - For example, I got the Ship card when my mother was Crossing over (Coffin + Ship)

IN A RELATIONSHIP:

- A long-distance relationship.
    - For example: when I was living in Germany, my boyfriend was in the US, and I got the Ship + Heart or Ship + Ring - we had a long-distance relationship for a while.

- It could be a romantic trip - it depends on what cards are around it
    - For example, in one of my daily draws, I pulled Ship + Anchor + Sun = that day, my boyfriend took me to the beach

- If negative cards are around the Ship and the Ship falls as the last card, it can mean leaving for good, breaking up, or a separation

- In relationship readings, I always look where the Ship is sailing toward (with directional reading - depending on the deck you are using, look where the Ship is sailing toward)
    - For example, Ship + Heart is positive, but the Ship going toward the Cross shows me the energy is going toward burdens and hardships

DESCRIBING A PERSON:

- An exotic-looking person (tanned/olive tone skin, dark hair, robust body type)

- A foreigner

- Somebody who travels a lot

- Depending on the question, it can talk about someone who is noncommittal (if surrounded by negative cards)

- An adventurer

HEALTH AND BODY PART:

- Liver, gall bladder, urinary tract, pancreas

- Ship + Fish + Whip can be alcoholism

MONEY:

- Money is coming in from trade and commerce

- Money is coming through a business

- Money is coming through inheritance, especially if the Coffin card is next to the Ship

- For me personally, it often meant money coming in from overseas transfers

ADVICE:

- Have the courage to do something

- Venture

- Be brave

- Enjoy freedom

- Try new things

OBJECTS:

- Ship, boat, car, train, any vehicle

TIMING:

- From 3 days to 3 months

- March

IN A GRAND TABLEAU, IF the Ship falls very close or close to the Significator card:

- Travel, Vacation (especially Stork + Ship combination)

- The Ship represents extra profits, for example, a financial windfall

- Winning money through gambling – especially If the Clover card is around!

- A windfall

- A gift of money – especially when the bouquet is around!

- A promotion at work

- Money coming in through inheritance – especially when the Coffin is around!

IN A GRAND TABLEAU, IF THE Ship is far or very far away from the Significator card:

- There will be no additional income

- No bonus

- No windfall

- The cards around the Ship will give you more information about the circumstances

Card Combination Examples:

- Some time ago, I asked the cards how my trip would go, and I got Ship + Mountain = I had a very frustrating delay

- After a disagreement, I asked the cards how my day would continue, and I got Whip + Ship + Bouquet = the Ship was sailing away from the discord (Whip) towards a happy turn of events (Bouquet)

- When I was moving houses, I got a House + Ship + Stork combination

Client Example:

Mary asked me: "Will John get back to me tonight?" Mary expected a call from John. So, I did a yes/no spread and pulled:

Moon + Fish + Ship =

Having the Ship as the last card tells me no. The Ship indicates going away. I pulled a clarifying card and got the Sun. That told me clearly that John would not call tonight but would definitely call tomorrow during the day.

Mary confirmed that John called the next day in the morning.

Chapter Eight

Card #4 - House - King of Hearts

When I go home
It's an easy way
To be grounded,
You learn to realize
What truly matters.
- Tony Stewart -

The House card #4 is a **neutral** card because it is influenced by the cards around it.

- The core meaning of the house is a **positive outcome in everything you do**
- It represents your **home, family**, real estate, a safe and secure place, stability, and comfort
- If positive cards surround the House card, it's a sign of prosperity
- Success
- Improvements

IN A RELATIONSHIP:

- Secure and stable relationship
- Moving in together
- Starting a family
- A comfortable relationship

DESCRIBING A PERSON:

- Sturdy looking
- Wide shoulders
- Well built
- This person likes to be at home, homey
- Grounded
- Calm
- A warm, friendly person
- Welcoming

HEALTH AND BODY PART:

- The body
- The bones
- Shoulders
- Depending on the context, a health reading can describe a stable condition, or it can suggest staying at home and resting

MONEY:

- The financial situation is safe and stable
- Money could come in through a family member

ADVICE:

- Be yourself
- Be comfortable
- Build a foundation

OBJECTS:

- A house
- An apartment
- Real Estate
- In health readings, it could be a small doctor's office or any other health-related building

TIMING:

- 4 days, 4 weeks, up to 1 month
- April

IN A GRAND TABLEAU, IF the House card falls close or very close to the Significator card:

It's a sign of prosperity, success, and improvement if there are no negative cards around

If the House card lands under the Significator card (Man/Woman card) in the middle of the Grand Tableau, that's a sign that the Significator has to be very careful of the people around him/her, especially if negative cards are surrounding the house like Snake, Fox or Mice.

IN A GRAND TABLEAU, IF the House card falls far or very far from the Significator card:

This means that the Man/Woman doesn't feel comfortable at home. The further away the House card is, the less control the Significator has. Look at what's around the House card to see what's going on in the Significator's home life.

IN A GRAND TABLEAU, if the House card lands in the house of the Tower and the Tower card lands in the house of the House, that could mean there will be a move, change, or separation.

NOTE: THE HOUSE CARD IS ONE OF THE TREE CARDS! **THE TREE CARDS ARE** TREE, HOUSE, GARDEN, CROSSROADS, and CHILD. IF ALL OF THE TREE CARDS FALL TOGETHER IN A GRAND TABLEAU, IT MEANS WISHES COME TRUE AND A BRIGHT FUTURE AWAITS!

A client of mine once had all 5 tree cards together in the Grand Tableau, and she entered a very prosperous time in her life.

Card Combination Examples:

- Snake + House + Whip = My client had a very nasty argument at home
- House + Stork = A move
- Ring + House + Heart + Stars = Lots of love and harmony in the house
- House + Mice = Stressful family matter
- House + Cross = A heavily burdened atmosphere at home

Chapter Nine

Card #5 - Tree - 7 of Hearts

*If you would know strength and patience,
welcome the company of trees.*

- Hal Borland -

The Tree card #5 is a **neutral** card. It is highly influenced by the surrounding cards.

- The core meaning of the Tree is **health and well-being**

- The Tree talks about health in general - our physical, mental, and spiritual health

- Look at the cards surrounding the Tree, and you will get a clear picture of one's health. Vibrant health is if positive cards are around the Tree, and poor health is if negative cards touch the Tree.

- In my readings, the Tree always came up as longevity and lifelong (like the Tower card)

- **Growth**

- **Patience**

- Endurance

- Fertility

- Slow but steady growth

- Deep-rooted

- Holding on

- Branching out

- It talks about patience

- Grounding

NOTE: There are readers out there who say the Tree card is, in general, a negative card. For me, this is absolutely not true!! **The Tree is only negative IN A GRAND TABLEAU IF it falls very close or close to the Significator.** If other negative cards like Coffin and Whip are touching it and having the Tower far away from the Significator and the Clouds touching the Tower, especially the dark side. In that case, it's a very unfavorable health combination.

Whatever you tell your cards to do or to represent, they will do it! It is up to you…If the Tree is negative for you, then it is so for you.

IN A RELATIONSHIP:

- It's a strong, deeply rooted relationship

- Soul mates

- A calm, peaceful, and untroubled relationship

- It's a serious love that lasts a lifetime (like Tower)

- Longevity, this relationship will last; it's a long-term one

- You need patience...

  - For example, my client Lisa asked: "When will I move in with my boyfriend?" I got the Tree several times. That means it will take time; she needs to have patience. Outcome: It took 5 years before Lisa moved in with her boyfriend.

DESCRIBING A PERSON:

- A grounded person

- A spiritual person

- Healthy

- Religious

- A balanced person

- Could be a nurse

- Green eyes

- A tall person

HEALTH AND BODY PART:

- The brain

- Mental health

- In a health reading, the Tree also represents oxygen and genetic disorders. It can suggest resting.

- When having the Tree, in combination with some other negative health cards, such as, the Coffin and the Whip, should alarm one to pay attention to one's health.

- In a health context, it could be a heart disease (Heart #24 + Tree #5 + Coffin #8). I got this combination for two of my clients; I told them to get a checkup, so they did. Two months later, both of my clients told me they were diagnosed with a heart disease.

MONEY:

- Money is growing slowly but steadily, like investments
- The financial situation is stable, but it always depends on the cards around the Tree

ADVICE:

- Be patient
- Ground yourself
- Meditate
- Grow
- Become established

OBJECTS:

- A tree
- Forests
- Family tree
- A chart
- Anything that looks like a tree or has a tree shape. For example, a lamp that looks

like a tree.

TIMING:

- It will take a long time - be patient!

- Up to 5 years (a tree needs a long time to grow!)

- May

Many of my female clients ask me: "Is this man I am with my partner for life?" **IN A GRAND TABLEAU, IF the Man card lands in the house of the Tree,** then that is a sign that this man is a life partner. But if the Man card was in the house of the Clover, that shows it is not a partner for life because the clover is short-lived.

IN A GRAND TABLEAU, IF the Tree is very close or close to the Significator card (Man/Woman card):

It means that he/she needs to pay attention to health matters. It's always a red flag if the Tree is touching the Significator. **ESPECIALLY IF THE COFFIN CARD IS TOUCHING THE TREE...** Then, I advise my client to get a checkup at the doctor's office. It is best to have the Tree far away from the Significator and surrounded by positive cards.

IN A GRAND TABLEAU, IF the Tree is far or very far from the Significator card, it's a positive sign for his/her well-being.

NOTE: THE TREE CARD IS ONE OF THE TREE CARDS! **THE TREE CARDS ARE** TREE, HOUSE, GARDEN, CROSSROADS, and CHILD.

IF ALL OF THE TREE CARDS FALL TOGETHER IN A GRAND TABLEAU, IT MEANS WISHES COME TRUE AND A BRIGHT FUTURE AWAITS!

PLEASE ALSO NOTE: THE TREE CARD IS ALSO ONE OF THE HEALTH GROUP CARDS.

The **HEALTH GROUP CONSIST OF THESE 5 CARDS:** TREE, COFFIN, WHIP, CLOUDS AND TOWER. If this Health Group of cards is close to the Significator, it is a very unfavorable health situation.

Having the Tower close to the Significator and surrounded by positive cards means a long, healthy life. But if the Tower is far from the Significator and the clouds are touching the Tower (especially with the dark side of the clouds), the health situation is not good.

Card Combination Examples:

- Tree + Garden = Vibrant health

- Tree + Clover = Recovering from illness

- Tree + Scythe = Operation, a fracture

- Interpretations for Heart + Tree = Depending on the context, if it's a relationship reading, it means growing love (my client Linda confirmed this after 5 years…the couple is still together and in a happy and serious relationship).

Client Example:

Here's an example of a daily draw I did for a client:

Tree + Coffin + Whip + Ship + Snake + Incense burner + Lilies

When I saw this line of cards, I knew immediately something negative would happen with my client's health today since Tree + Coffin + Whip = are Health cards. It turns out my client had an accident in her office… She smashed her finger with a drawer and was injured and in pain for a couple of weeks.

How I interpreted this line: The Coffin, in this scenario, represents the drawer, and the Whip stands for pain. The Ship shows us where the energy is flowing. It's going towards the Snake, indicating health problems and complications that won't last long.

The Incense burner shows us that the problems the Snake is causing will be cleared away, and as the last card, we have the Lilies, which tells us all will be well in the end, but patience is required!

Personal Example:

Here is a personal story; this was one of my daily draws:

Tree + Ring + Woman + Rider + Whip

The first card is the tree, which stands for health, so I knew something would be going on with health/well-being.

The Ring next to the tree told me it was something repetitive, a pattern.

The Woman card represents me.

The Rider stands for legs in a health context.

The Whip was another indication that it's something repetitive and can also stand for a muscle.

Interpretation: The outcome of this daily draw was an old hamstring injury I have flared up again.

Chapter Ten

Card #6 - Clouds - King of Clubs

Worries are like clouds that pass through the mind.

The Cloud card # 6 is a **negative** card.

- The core meaning of the Clouds is **trouble**

- This is the card that represents **confusion**

- **Sour air!** - a very unpleasant atmosphere

- Nothing is clear...you can't see...

- Problems and complications

- Trouble

- Uncertainties

- Doubts

- Unhappy events

IN A RELATIONSHIP:

- Having doubts about the relationship

- Being confused about the relationship

- The feeling of being lost, not knowing what's going on

- Misunderstandings

- Troubles

DESCRIBING A PERSON:

- Grumpy

- A troublemaker

- Drama queen

- Moody, mood swings

- Irritated

- Confused person

- A smoker

- Has an attitude

- Gray hair

- Light blue to grey eyes

HEALTH AND BODY PART:

- The lungs, respiratory system

- In health readings, the Clouds stand for asthma, bronchitis, pneumonia, colds, and smoker's lung

- Also came up in my readings as depression

- Being under the influence of something inhaled

MONEY:

- Financial troubles

- Financial worries

ADVICE:

- Clear your mind

- Step back and detach from the circumstances

- Think before you talk!

- Focus

- Don't reveal everything

OBJECTS:

- Everything that has to do with smoke or producing smoke

- Fog

- Cigarettes

- Incense
- Diffuser, humidifier

TIMING:

- Autumn
- June
- 6 days, 6 weeks, 6 months

IN A GRAND TABLEAU, IF the Clouds are on top of the Significator, this has the most negative impact.

An ideal situation is for the Clouds to be as far away as possible to the left and underneath, with the light side turned towards the Significator (Please note: Depending on which card deck you use, the light and the dark side of the clouds vary in each card deck).

IN A GRAND TABLEAU, if the dark side of the Clouds faces the Significator, troubles and unpleasant events are coming.

The dark side has the strongest negative impact. If the light side of the clouds faces the Significator, it is less problematic and less dramatic than the other way around. Especially if positive cards like the Sun or the Key follow the Clouds, trouble is on the way out. The Sun card has the power to neutralize the negative effects of the Clouds.

ALSO IN A GRAND TABLEAU:

- The Clouds card is a very unpleasant card to have near the Significator. It can bring misfortune and can eliminate the positive effects of the good cards.
- As I described earlier, it's always best to have the Clouds as far to the left as possible and underneath the Significator with the light side turned towards him/her.
- A very unfavorable position of the Clouds would be directly over the Significator's head. That shows that the Man/Woman is confused, doesn't think clearly, and has a lot of troubles on his/her mind.

- The old tradition says if the King is facing the Significator card, it's a good omen. But if the King has his back to the Significator, then unpleasant events are on the way.

- I look at which house the Clouds landed. This shows me where the trouble is coming from.

- Always examine if the Clouds are touching any Life Area cards, such as the House card (family), Heart and Ring (relationship), the work card, and Child (Children). Then, you can prepare the client to be cautious in these areas.

Card Combination Examples:

- Clouds + Sun = Things are getting better
- Clouds + Key = Solutions are found

But if a negative card follows the Clouds, then the troubles are enhanced. For example:

- Clouds + Snake = Danger, lies
- Clouds + Mountain = Nothing good, a failure, confusing delays
- Clover + Clouds = Grief, sadness
- Lily + Clouds = Family grief, sorrow
- Stars + Clouds = Uncertain situation, many sad circumstances
- Letter + Clouds = Problematic message/letter
- Tower + Clouds = Illness and even death (depending on the other card constellations)
- Dog + Clouds = Disloyal friend
- Crossroads + Clouds = Hesitation, uncertain decision, stormy weather on one's path

NOTE:

Clouds clear out quickly...sunshine after the storm!

Stay positive, and pay attention to your thoughts!

Chapter Eleven

Card #7 - Snake- Queen of Clubs

No matter how many times a Snake sheds its skin, it will always be a Snake.

The Snake card #7 is a **negative** card.

- The core meaning of the Snake is **betrayal**
- It means danger

- Problems, complications, and difficulties

- Harmful people or circumstances

- Deceit, scam

- Disaster

- Jealous people are around, and envy

- Lies and betrayal

- Disloyal people are around - be careful whom you trust

IN A RELATIONSHIP:

- Dishonesty

- Unfaithful

- Not telling the truth

- Jealousy

- Cheating

- Betrayal

- Depending on the context, the question, and the surrounding cards, the Snake came up in my readings very often as **seduction**

DESCRIBING A PERSON:

- Sexy

- Slim

- Shady

- Able to move quickly and easily

- A jealous person

- A sweet talker and backstabber
- Talks behind your back
- Undependable

HEALTH AND BODY PART:

- Virus
- A light cold or flu (something easy to recover from unless other negative cards follow)
- The colon, large intestines.
    - For example, in one of my client's health readings, I got Mountain + Snake = Constipation
- In a health context, the Snake can also talk about poison and could represent medications
- Worms
- All kinds of addictions, especially when the Whip is around
- Skin problems like very dry skin

MONEY:

- Financial difficulties
- A loss of money
- Don't lend money!
- Not a good time for investments

ADVICE:

- Pay attention to the people around you and be careful whom you trust
- Be clever

- Use your intelligence
- Do things not the usual way - for example, do things a different way

Client Example:

To understand "do things a different way" better, I will tell you the story of my client, Alex. Alex had been searching for a job for a couple of months and sent out his resume by mail and email without any response. So, he came to me for advice, and I asked the cards: "What can Alex do differently to get a response from the employer?" I pulled:

Crossroads + Snake + Letter

Immediately, I knew Alex had to deliver his resume in a different way. I told him to drop it off in person instead of sending it by mail and introduce himself. A couple of weeks later, Alex gave me feedback that my advice worked, and he landed an interview.

OBJECTS:

- Necklace
- Bracelet
- Chain
- Wires
- Cables
- Pipes, drains
- Anything that looks snaky

TIMING:

- 7 days, 7 weeks, 7 months
- July

IN A GRAND TABLEAU, IF the Snake card lands in the house of the Scythe, there is serious danger and complications.

IN A GRAND TABLEAU, IF THE SNAKE IS VERY CLOSE OR CLOSE TO THE SIGNIFICATOR:

Lies, betrayal, and losses are around the corner. Pay attention to your surroundings! Check if there are any person cards next to the Snake...that might be a malicious person. From my experience, where the head of the Snake is pointing is where the betrayal is coming from. Also, always check in which house the Snake is sitting in. For example, the Snake in the house of the House card #4 tells you the problems have to do with family matters. If very positive cards like the Key or Sun follow the Snake, the Snake can be neutralized, and you will find a way to go around the Snake. If the Coffin appears after the Snake, that means the problems will end, but look at which card follows after the Coffin. If it's a positive card, it will be favorable, but if it's a negative card, the negativity is prolonged.

IN A GRAND TABLEAU, IF THE SNAKE IS FAR OR VERY FAR:

It is always good to have the Snake as far as possible from the Significator. That way, there's no danger. But check if there are any Life Area cards around the Snake card! The Snake will cause trouble in the Life Areas it's touching.

Life Area Cards:

- **Tree** = Health
- **Heart** = Love
- **Ring** = Relationships
- **House** = Family, Private life
- **Dog** = Friends or a partner
- **Fox** or **Market** (#40 from the Rana George Lenormand deck) = Work
- **Child** = Children
- **Ship** = Travel
- **Book** = Study, school, a project

- **Garden** = Social circle, environment

- **Fish** = Money flow, receiving money

- **Bear** = All financial matters

Card Combination Examples:

- Snake + Coffin = End of problems

- Snake + Sun = An enemy is defeated

- Snake + Coffin + Fox = This is a very negative combination that leads to betrayal, lies, and losses

Personal Examples:

A quick personal story about the Snake. Several times, I got the same card constellation:

Scythe + Dog + Snake

It played out that a friend was hiding ill feelings about me, and while playing nice in front of me, she double-crossed me.

The Snake can also describe a detour. Here is another example: A couple of years ago, I went on a bike ride, and I had to make a detour because of construction, which caused a long delay. These were the cards I pulled on that day:

Rider + Snake + Mountain

The Rider represents the bike, the Snake is the detour, and the Mountain is the delay.

Chapter Twelve
Card #8 - Coffin - 9 of Diamonds

THE LENORMAND

If you want to escape from your cage, you must die while you are alive.

- Ancient Parable -

Death is not the greatest loss in life. The greatest loss is what dies inside us while we live.

- Norman Cousins -

The Coffin card #8 is a **negative** card.

- The core meaning of the Coffin is **death, illness, and loss**
- It talks about endings and illness
- Sadness, depression
- Serious loss, financial losses
- Very draining, depressing circumstances
- Painful transformations

- In daily draws, the effect of the Coffin is diminished. It could simply mean going to bed or resting
- The state of not flowing or moving - stagnation

IN A RELATIONSHIP:

- Separation, divorce
- An emotionally painful relationship
- Sorrow
- The relationship is dying or dead

DESCRIBING A PERSON:

- A negative person
- A pessimist
- A sick person
- A depressed person
- Feeling down and unhappy
- No self-esteem
- A cold, heartless person
- Tired looking
- Grumpy
- Dark hair
- Dark eyes
- A square looking jawline

HEALTH AND BODY PART:

- The Coffin stands for disease in general
- The illness is getting worse
- Bedridden
- Depression
- Headache
- Could represent an MRI
- Claustrophobia
- Fatigue

Client Example:

One of my dear clients suffered from cancer. I always got the identical card combination for the cancer: Mountain + Mice + Coffin.

NOTE: When you see Tree + Coffin, that's a red flag. I usually recommend seeing a doctor. It could be a serious illness or severe depression - depending on the other card constellations.

MONEY:

- Bankruptcy (Fish + Coffin)
- A big financial loss

ADVICE:

- It's time to rest
- Lie down

OBJECTS:

- A box
- A drawer

- A closet
- A cellar, basement
- A bed
- Anything that has a lid

TIMING:

- Eternity
- Never
- 8 days, 8 weeks, 8 months
- August

IN A GRAND TABLEAU, IF COFFIN IS VERY CLOSE OR CLOSE TO THE SIGNIFICATOR:

- **A loss** of health, money, or any material loss (like losing a house)
- Feeling bad, depression
- Headaches
- A crisis
- Fatigue
- Powerlessness
- An ending (once again, look at the card that comes BEFORE the Coffin because that's the subject that's ending). Hopefully, the card before the Coffin is negative.
- If Coffin is very close or close, see where the other health cards (Tree, Whip, and Tower) are located to get confirmation if the Coffin is health-related

IN A GRAND TABLEAU, IF COFFIN IS FAR OR VERY FAR FROM THE

THE LENORMAND

SIGNIFICATOR:

It's good to have the Coffin as far as possible from the Significator card. In terms of health, it's positive to have the Coffin at a distance. But check which cards, especially which Life Area cards, the Coffin is touching.

IN A GRAND TABLEAU, look at the card that comes before the Coffin…the card before the Coffin is the topic of what's ending. It's always good to have a negative card BEFORE the Coffin card because the Coffin ENDS the problems and complications of that card. Then look what's coming after the Coffin. If a positive card follows the Coffin, that is good. But if a negative card follows the Coffin, that is not so good; it prolongs the negative effects of the Coffin.

IN A GRAND TABLEAU, the house of the Coffin shows what the serious problem of the Significator is. For example, if the Clouds card lands in the house of the Coffin, that means the Significator has fears and insecurities, which are serious problems.

IN A GRAND TABLEAU, IF the Snake card lands in the house of the Coffin, that means the problems and complications will end.

Card Combination Examples:

- Coffin + Snake = This could be a dangerous enemy and negative influences

- Coffin + Sun = Happy ending, success after an ending

- Coffin + Bouquet = Happiness returns after an ending

- Mountain + Coffin + Child = The Coffin is ending the problems (Mountain), and after the Coffin, there is a new beginning (Child)

- Coffin + Crossroads = A new direction

- Coffin + Stars = A positive transformation

- Coffin + Clouds = Depression

- Coffin + Stork = A big change can also indicate a move (moving house)

- Coffin + Moon = Very painful feelings, negative emotions, being mentally tired and very down

- Coffin + Cross = Sadness and deep pain
- Coffin + Key = Solutions are found, and misfortune ends

Client example:

My client Jane asked: "Will my boyfriend Lee come back?" I performed a simple yes/no 3-card spread:

Snake + Coffin + Clover

Answer: Yes, there will be a reconciliation!

Interpretation:

Snake = Problems & Complications. The Coffin ENDS the problems and complications of the Snake because it's a negative card BEFORE the Coffin card.

Coffin + Clover is always a reconciliation, a second chance. If a negative card follows the Coffin, it prolongs the negativity of the Coffin.

Personal Example:

Before my mother passed away, I got Coffin + Ship and Coffin + Scythe. This combination could stand for death, especially if other negative cards like the Cross are around.

Chapter Thirteen

Card #9 - Bouquet - Queen of Spades

A flower does not think of competing with the flowers next to it. it just blooms.

- Zen Shin -

The Bouquet card #9 is a **positive** card.

- The core meaning of the Bouquet is **happiness** and **joy**

- Satisfaction

- A pleasant surprise

- A gift

- A beautiful offer of something

- Anything that has to do with beauty

- Acknowledgment

- An award

- The Bouquet also stands for gratitude and appreciation

- If you are in need, someone will help

- A happy turn of events

NOTE: Having the Bouquet after a negative card announces the end of trouble and worries. But if a negative card follows the Bouquet, it warns of disappointments and unpleasant situations.

IN A RELATIONSHIP:

- A flourishing, happy relationship

- Satisfaction

- Peace and harmony

- There's no imbalance of power - partners respect each other

- In a relationship, reading Bouquet + Ring could be a wedding proposal.

DESCRIBING A PERSON:

- A beautiful, attractive person

- Light hair (blond, light brown)

- Light skin tone

- A happy person

- A very likable, pleasant person

- Lovely and enjoyable person

- Anything that has to do with beauty, for example, a cosmetician or make-up artist

HEALTH AND BODY PART:

- In a health context, the Bouquet stands for allergies, especially pollen allergies

- Having the Bouquet at the end of a health line reading means recovery and healing

- It can also talk about aesthetic medicine; beauty surgery (Scythe + Bouquet)

- Hyperpigmentation of the skin

- In a health reading, having the Bouquet next to the Tree card indicates healing and good health.

MONEY:

- Nothing to worry about!

- Unexpected income (A gift of money)

- Financial situation is safe

- A positive outcome

- In a money reading, the Bouquet + Fish combination represents a gift of money, a good investment, or a windfall.

ADVICE:

- Be grateful

- Show appreciation
- Be happy and joyful
- Beautify (for example, your home, yourself)

OBJECTS:

- A bouquet
- Flowers
- Anything that has to do with beauty (Skincare, Makeup)
- Art
- A beautiful painting
- A gift

TIMING:

- Spring
- 9 days, 9 months
- September

Client Example:

A client asked me once: "When will I move?" I pulled;

House + Stork + Anchor + Bouquet = I charged the last card in this line to be the answer for the timing.

House + Stork = This is a classical combination that indicates a move

Stork + Anchor talks about settling elsewhere

And the last card, our outcome, is the Bouquet

My answer was: You will be moving in the spring

My client later confirmed this.

IN A GRAND TABLEAU, IF THE BOUQUET IS VERY CLOSE OR CLOSE TO THE SIGNIFICATOR:

When the Bouquet falls very close or close, it's always a lucky sign. Something good will fall into your lap...Something will bring you happiness and joy; it may be a gift or an invitation. Gratitude and appreciation are coming your way. Suppose the Bouquet and Lilies fall together very close or close to the Significator. In that case, that's a sign that the Significator will be rewarded for his/her goodness, especially if the Lilies card is above the Significator's head (I'll go into detail about this later in the Lilies chapter).

IN A GRAND TABLEAU, IF THE BOUQUET IS FAR OR VERY FAR FROM THE SIGNIFICATOR:

In these positions, the Bouquet has no negative impact. The Significator just won't get any beneficial extras in life if the Bouquet is far or very far. But the Bouquet will still have a beneficial effect on its surrounding cards. Always check if the Bouquet is touching any Life Area cards (Tree, Heart, Ring, House, Dog, Fox or Market, Child, Ship, Book, Garden, Fish, Bear).

Card Combination Example:

- Child + Book + Bouquet = Whenever I got this card constellation, it was about some new information that brings happiness. The Child card here stands for something new, and the Book card talks about information/knowledge.

Chapter Fourteen

Card #10 - Scythe - Jack of Diamonds

As soon as there is life,
there is danger.
- Ralph Waldo Emerson -

The Scythe card #10 is a **negative** card, but sometimes it is **neutral** (depending on the surrounding cards…It may be neutral when it's about a decision).

- Any card that lands before the Scythe is being cut; the Scythe can neutralize negative and positive cards that land before it

- The core meaning of the Scythe is **danger**
- The Scythe has to do with endings, a separation
- It's an action card
- Decisive action
- Sudden and quick decisions
- It clears, cuts away
- Could be a warning about danger
- With other negative cards like Coffin, it can mean an accident
- With positive cards around, it can talk about uncertainties, insecurities, and fears
- Whatever the Scythe brings is sudden and unexpected
- Depending on the context and what cards are around, it can also be about pain

IN A RELATIONSHIP:

- A breakup, separation, divorce
- Emotional pain
- Rejection
- Cutting of
- Can be an ending of a dangerous relationship

DESCRIBING A PERSON:

- Could be an aggressive person
- Strong

- A person with a sharp mind who's acting quickly
- A fast person
- A hairdresser
- A surgeon, a dentist
- Could be slim with some curves
- Often tattoos

HEALTH AND BODY PART:

- Teeth pain (together with the Mice)
- Injuries
- Any kind of stabbing pain (Headache, Tooth pain, etc.)
- Cuts
- Scars
- Fractures, broken bones
- Injections
- Surgery
- Anything that involves sharp instruments and needles
- Years ago, I did a health reading for a client, and I remember I got very close to the Tree: Scythe + Mice = which turned out to be a toothache
- As I mentioned earlier, with the Bouquet card next to the Scythe, it can be plastic surgery

MONEY:

- Financial cut

- The money flow will stop unexpectedly, and all of a sudden
- A crisis like economic collapse, stock crash
- Salary cut
- Decrease in compensation
- In a financial reading, whenever I get Fish + Scythe, it always talks about a financial cut or financial crisis

ADVICE:

- Declutter
- Be sharp
- Make a decision
- Be determined
- Be forceful
- Be exact and accurate

OBJECTS:

- Anything that's sharp and can cut
- Knives
- Needles
- Scissors
- Tools (like gardening tools)

TIMING:

- It's going to happen very suddenly and unexpectedly
- 10 days, 10 months

- The fall season

- October

NOTE: If the Man/Woman card appears before the Scythe, it means the person makes a very quick/sharp decision.

IN A GRAND TABLEAU, IF THE SCYTHE IS VERY CLOSE OR CLOSE TO THE SIGNIFICATOR CARD:

The Scythe in these positions causes danger, threatens the Significator's well-being, and causes great insecurities. Look closely at which Life Area cards are touching the Scythe and which card is before the Scythe. Every card that comes before the Scythe is being cut.

Also, check the Health Group constellation (Tree, Coffin, Whip, Tower, Clouds). If the Health Group is close, it could threaten one's health and well-being. It can be an injury or surgery. If positive cards are around the Scythe, it could be a decision that has to be made to move forward. Very positive cards can eliminate the danger or make the Scythe less severe; they soften its effects - in that case, I read the Scythe as fear.

If negative cards are around the Scythe, severe suffering and troubles are expected. It can also be a difficult, unpleasant decision that comes with sacrifices.

IN A GRAND TABLEAU, IF THE SCYTHE IS FAR OR VERY FAR FROM THE SIGNIFICATOR:

It is always positive and safe to have the Scythe far away from the Man/Woman card. In these placements, it cannot harm him/her. But pay attention to which cards are being affected by the Scythe. Are there any Life Area cards touching the Scythe? For example, the Fish card represents the Life Area of finances. If the Scythe follows the Fish, it may be a financial cut.

Card Combinations Examples:

- Ship + Scythe = A cancelled trip. It could also be an accident (this depends on what other cards are around).

- Scythe + Crossroads = A separation, a sudden change, a sudden decision (context and the surrounding cards are very important).

- Scythe + Lilies = Means that one's peace will be very disturbed. A client of mine got this combination several times, and it played out to be a very unpleasant family matter with many disagreements.

Client Example:

This was a daily draw for a friend of mine, I pulled:

Ship + Snake + Scythe = The Ship shows where the energy is flowing / where the journey is going...

The Snake here represents problems and complications, and the Scythe told me something unexpected would happen - nothing pleasant. It turns out my friend went on a bike ride and got a flat tire. I am always amazed at how literal the cards can be! The Snake in this reading is the tire. At the bike repair shop, they told my friend somebody had cut or punctured the tire!

Chapter Fifteen

Card #11 - Whip - Jack of Clubs

There is no person so severely punished as those who subject themselves to the Whip of their own remorse.

- Seneca -

The Whip is a **negative** card, but it can be **neutral - it depends on the context and the surrounding cards.**

THE LENORMAND

- The core meaning of the Whip is **discord**

- The Whip talks about repetitive motion, for example, any physical activity like cleaning, exercising, practicing dancing, etc.

- Doing something over and over again, like editing or writing

- Restarting something over and over again

- Discussions: back-and-forth communication (the type of communication - good or bad - depends on the surrounding cards.)

- It can be an argument like a back-and-forth debate

- Discord with friends, family, or other relationships, for example, at work

- Punishment

- Violence, fights, anger

- Problems and troubles with people

- Sex

- Passionate

- In a health context, it stands for a repetitive health issue, a chronic disease, something that flares up over and over again

- The Whip card is one of the Health Group cards (Tree, Coffin, Whip, Tower, Clouds)

NOTE:

The context is important - the question you ask and the surrounding cards. The Whip can be very negative like physical abuse, OR something very pleasant. As I mentioned earlier, I love to use the Rana George Lenormand deck because she has 4 extra cards; one of them is the BED card #39. The Bed card frees the Whip from the sex subject. If you don't have the Rana George deck, then I would charge the Whip card in my mind, depending on the context and what it's supposed to represent.

HOW TO CHARGE A CARD

For example, if you want the Whip card to represent sex, then you say it in your mind while you're shuffling the cards. Another example is the Significator cards - Man (#28) and Woman (#29) cards. If your client's name is Mary, then you think about the Woman card #29 to represent Mary, and Mary's boyfriend Peter is represented by card 28, the Man. You charge the cards while shuffling and think about nothing else. After you have done that, you ask your question and continue shuffling.

Another example is if you want to ask about a certain friend, then you would charge the Dog card #18 to represent that specific friend. This process is very important! Otherwise, you will have difficulties interpreting who is who.

IN A RELATIONSHIP:

- A very passionate relationship
- Physical relationship
- Lots of sex
- Lots of emotions that can be difficult to control
- A quarrelsome relationship
- Disagreements
- Tensions

DESCRIBING A PERSON:

- Likes to argue
- Wants to be right
- Aggressive
- Likes to compete
- Intense

- Showing intense feelings

- Sexy

- In shape

- Muscular

- A bodybuilder

- Could have a loud voice

HEALTH AND BODY PART:

- Fever

- Pain

- A chronic condition

- Recurring issues

- A long-term illness

- Fertility

- Inflammations

- ADHD

- Infections

- The male organ

- Muscles

MONEY:

- Hard times with money

- Argument because of money

- Unsatisfying result

- A payment that's occurring again several times in the same way

ADVICE:

- Be peaceful

- THINK before you speak and take action

- Work out, be physical

- Do something again

- Retry, repeat

- Practice more

- Discuss

OBJECTS:

- Anything that can be used for sweeping, for example, a broom

- A brush

- Whip

- A strip of leather

- A belt

- A rope

- Any type of band, for example, exercise bands

TIMING:

- 11 days, 11 weeks, 11 months

- November

IN A GRAND TABLEAU, IF THE WHIP IS VERY CLOSE OR CLOSE TO THE SIGNIFICATOR:

If it falls very close or close, it causes a lot of discord and disharmony. Unpleasant, heated discussions and arguments may come up. Always examine the surrounding cards to see where the quarrel is coming from and who is involved. If negative cards are around the Whip, the tensions will be heightened. If positive cards are around, the troubles will be solved faster. Solutions will be found.

The Significator will deal with frustrations and disappointments in his/her private life or work life (once again, the surrounding cards will give you insight from where and from whom the disruption of harmony is coming). Check where the rest of the Health Group is (Tree, Coffin, Clouds, and Tower). Having the Whip close may be an illness - how severe will be shown by the Health Group cards and other surrounding cards.

IN A GRAND TABLEAU, IF THE WHIP IS FAR OR VERY FAR FROM THE SIGNIFICATOR:

In these positions, the Whip does not harm the Significator. However, the Whip influences the cards it touches. Therefore, examine which Life Area cards the Whip touches.

Client examples:

In a money context:

My client Linda asked me once if her financial situation would improve within the next 6 months. I pulled:

Fish + Whip + Coffin + Key + Sun

I love it when the cards affirm the question. In this example, we see clearly that her financial situation (Fish) is a struggle; she has hard times with money (Fish + Whip), but this hardship will end (Coffin), and the solution (Key) and big success (Sun) are coming.

After 6 months, I followed up with Linda. She gave me feedback that, indeed, her finances improved.

In a relationship context:

Another reading I did for a client was about a get-together with her boyfriend. These cards flew out:

Ring + Fox + Whip + Bouquet + Heart =

The Ring here shows it is about the relationship.

When I saw the Fox, I knew something would go wrong.

The Whip was an argument, but it ended very pleasantly (Bouquet + Heart)!

When I get the Bouquet + Heart combination in a relationship context, I know there's true love.

Chapter Sixteen

Card #12 - Birds - 7 of Diamonds

The biggest communication problem is we do not listen to understand.
We listen to reply.

The Birds card #12 is a **neutral** card. It is highly influenced by the surrounding cards.

- The Birds card is all about **communication**

- Verbal communication like phone calls, voice messages

- Any electronic communications like text messages, tweets, any social media communications

- Wi-Fi

- Meeting

- Interview

- A date

- Siblings

- A couple

- Distractions

- Little annoyances that are short-lived

NOTE:

Going by the traditional Lenormand meanings, the core meaning of the birds is **stress.** But I disagree with that when very positive cards are surrounding the birds. It all depends on your question, the context, and how you charge the cards. In my long years of reading the cards, I was never wrong in interpreting the Birds card. But if the Birds mean stress for you, then it is so for you - in other words, whatever you tell your cards with your mind to represent, they will do it and adjust!

IN A RELATIONSHIP:

- This is my couple card, lovers

- Two people being together

- A date

- Loving conversations

- In a relationship reading, if I get the Bird card BEFORE the Man/Woman card, that tells me this person is in a relationship already

DESCRIBING A PERSON:

- Communicative
- Chatty
- Gossipy
- An expressive person
- Public speaker
- Small piercing eyes
- High-pitched and very sharp voice

HEALTH AND BODY PART:

- Vocal cords
- Throat
- The nerves
- Nervousness
- Tensions
- Blood pressure
- Hot flashes

MONEY:

- The stock markets
- Money can come in through communications

ADVICE:

- Communicate

- Make that contact through any form of communication
- Raise one's voice
- Speak up

OBJECTS:

- Birds
- A phone
- Anything that has to do with music
- Any object that plays music (radio, iPod, etc.)

TIMING:

- 12 days, 12 weeks, up to 1 year
- December
- In my readings, I've noticed most of the time, it was around 3 months, and sometimes the Spring. Timing is a little tricky! I would pull a clarifying card to help.

WHAT IS A CLARIFYING CARD?

Let me give you an easy example from a daily draw I did for a friend. I pulled 5 cards for her:

Stork + Clover + Scythe + Key + Birds

This Line of 5 looks very positive except for the Focus Card that's in the middle: the Scythe. I wanted to get more insight about the Scythe card, so I reshuffled the cards while I left the 5 cards on the table, and I asked in my mind: "Why is the Scythe card here?" When I did that, a card jumped out of the deck while I was shuffling. That's when I knew there was my answer: I got the Woman card #29 as the clarifier, and then I knew my friend had made a sharp decision or cut something off... It turned out that my friend received a phone call, but she decided not to answer. Later, she called back and had a positive conversation (Key 33 + Birds 12).

IN A GRAND TABLEAU, IF THE BIRDS ARE VERY CLOSE OR CLOSE TO THE SIGNIFICATOR CARD:

In the old traditional instructions, the Birds in these positions announce little troubles, annoyances, or stresses that are easily overcome and short-lived. BUT for me, the surrounding cards highly influence the Birds. In other words, positive cards around the Birds make the Birds a positive card, so the communication is positive. But if the Birds are surrounded by very challenging cards, the Birds become negative, such as negative gossip. Also, what subject the Birds represent always depends on your question, the context, and the cards that are touching the Birds! Also, I've noticed in my readings that the Birds card can represent one's thoughts. What type of troubles or communications depends on the surrounding cards. Always check if there are any Life Area cards touching the Birds. That way, you know where the troubles or communications are coming from, and you can tell by the cards around the Birds what kind of communication it will be.

IN A GRAND TABLEAU, IF THE BIRDS ARE FAR OR VERY FAR FROM THE SIGNIFICATOR:

In these positions, the Birds may indicate a small trip if other card constellations support this, such as if the Ship lands close to the Man/Woman card.

IN A GRAND TABLEAU, IF the Birds card lands in the house of the Crossroads, it means there are conversations about the future or decisions... To get more insight into what the conversation is about, you would look at where the Crossroads landed. For example, if it's in the house of the Ring, it has to do with a relationship.

Card Combination Examples:

- Birds + Cross = Very negative, heavy conversations
- Birds + Clouds = Confusing conversations that lead to misunderstandings
- Birds + Tree = Conversations regarding health
- Birds + Key = Conversations that bring solutions, answers are found
- Birds + Crossroads = Talking about the future

- Birds + Fish = Financial discussion

- Birds + Coffin = No communication, not hearing back

- Birds + Mice = Stressful communications

- Birds + Child = Instagram

- Birds + Park = WhatsApp

- Birds + Book = Facebook

Client example:

Here is the story of my client, Jason. Jason wanted to know how his meeting with his new boss would go. I pulled:

Clover + Fish + Key + Lilies + Birds + Sun

Outcome: Jason's meeting with his new boss was very positive. He received a financial bonus, and they had a very long, satisfying conversation.

Clover + Fish = Financial abundance, being lucky with money matters

Fish + Key = Success regards money

Key + Lilies = Wisdom and patience is the key

Jason learned a lot during the conversation with his boss, but he had to practice patience because the meeting took a long time!

Lilies + Birds = A long, peaceful conversation that brings satisfaction

Birds + Sun = Successful, bright conversation with a positive outcome

Chapter Seventeen
Card #13 - Child - Jack of Spades

We keep moving forward,
Opening new doors,
And doing new things,
Because we're curious.
Curiosity keeps leading us
Down new paths.
- Walt Disney -

The Child card #13 is a **neutral** card. It is influenced by its surrounding cards.

- The core meaning of the Child is **EASE**

- The Child card talks about new beginnings

- A new and fresh start

- A new project

- Something new

- The Child card symbolizes innocence

- Trusting
- Spontaneous
- Playful
- Immature, naive
- Goodness
- Kindness
- The Child is a Life Area card that represents children

IN A RELATIONSHIP:

- A new relationship
- Being playful
- Going step by step - taking it slow because it's just starting
- This is a relationship where they can trust each other
- There is a lot of kindness and goodness between this couple

DESCRIBING A PERSON:

- A naive person
- Being childish
- Not mature
- Young looking
- Innocent looking
- Babyface, doll face
- Petite

- Trusting

- Playful

- Has not enough experience

- Impulsive, spontaneous, doing things unplanned

HEALTH AND BODY PART:

- Childhood diseases

- Pregnancy (with the Stork together)

- Small infection

- In a health context, it can talk about new medications, a new treatment, or a new opinion from a doctor

- Also, in a health context, it can refer to minimizing, shrinking, or becoming smaller.

MONEY:

- A small sum of money

- A new or small investment: For example, if we are doing a money reading, you ask: "How much money will I get?" When the Child card shows up, then, the amount is small.

ADVICE:

- Don't be so serious

- Be playful

- Have fun

- Be open-minded

- Trust more

THE LENORMAND

OBJECTS:

- Child, children
- Anything that has to do with children, for example, a playground or toys

TIMING:

- 13 days
- Up to 1 year

IN A GRAND TABLEAU, IF THE CHILD CARD IS VERY CLOSE OR CLOSE TO THE SIGNIFICATOR:

If the Child card is very close or close to the Man/Woman card, that shows me that the Significator is full of goodness and kindness towards everybody - it's a good-natured person - and that the Significator is surrounded by good company (good friends). Before I do a reading, I always ask if my client has any children. The Child card near can represent one's children. If there are negative cards around the Child, that means parenthood requires attention. Having the Child card close means you have control over the child. If the Stork, the Anchor, the Garden, the Tree, and the Moon are also close by, it can be a pregnancy.

If I do a reading for a client without children, the Child card in the very close and close positions can symbolize a new beginning, a new project, or something just starting. To get more insight, I look at the cards around the Child.

IN A GRAND TABLEAU, IF THE CHILD CARD IS FAR OR VERY FAR FROM THE SIGNIFICATOR:

In these positions, the Significator is not having very much fun in his/her life at the moment, and the kindness and goodness of the Significator go unnoticed. It could be that the Significator is not very pleasant to be around right now. If the Child card represents the Significator's child, that means that the Significator has not much control over his/her Child at the moment.

Card Combination Examples:

- Child + House = A small house, a new house

- Child + Rider = Could be a small move, a new start

- Child + Coffin = Can represent an abortion or a miscarriage

- Child + Scythe = Abortion

- Child + Garden = Playground

- Child + Fish = Small amount of money, or a small/new business

- Child + Tower = School

Client Example:

My client Margarethe had cancer, and we got the following cards:

Tree + Mice + Stars + Child + Sun

The Tree affirms the context. Mice + Stars stands for the cancer, and the Child says it's becoming smaller. The Sun is a very positive card, so I knew everything would be fine... Two weeks later, her doctor told her the cancer was shrinking.

Chapter Eighteen

Card #14 - Fox- Nine of Clubs

A fox is a wolf who sends flowers.
- Ruth Brown -

The Fox is a **negative** card, but if it is activated as a job card, it becomes **neutral**.

Some readers use the Moon or the Anchor to represent work, while other readers use the Fox card. I used to use the **Fox** because, in French cartomancy, the 9 of clubs symbolizes **work**. Now, I am using the Rana George Lenormand cards because she includes 4 extra cards. One of these extra cards is the **Market Card # 40**, which stands for work. That way, it frees the Fox from the work aspect.

In French cartomancy, the nine of clubs represents work. If I am doing a reading specifically regarding work, I charge/activate the Fox card in my mind to represent the job. Then I look to see which cards are around the Fox card. This gives me information about what's going on at the job. As I mentioned, I love to use the Rana George Lenormand deck because of her 4 extra cards; one is the Market #40, which stands for work. That way, the Fox is free from the work aspect.

- The core meaning of the Fox card is **wrongness**

- Watch out; something is wrong!

- It's a trap

- The Fox is all about manipulation, sneakiness, treachery, and stealth

- The Fox is very clever and a trickster

- Fraud

- The Fox is a hustler. He is always running around to bring food to the table, to survive, and to take care of his family.

- The Fox can also represent a person or how a person is acting

- It also talks about strategy and can advise you to investigate more

- If there are more negative cards surrounding the Fox, that is a warning. You have to be aware and prepared, especially if people are sweet-talking you.

IN A RELATIONSHIP:

- One of the parties is playing a game

- Something is wrong

- A secret or ulterior motive for something (a hidden agenda)

- Someone is hiding their real motives
- Manipulating somebody in a skillful manner
- Funny business going on, dishonesty

DESCRIBING A PERSON:

- Fit and in shape
- Fast
- Attractive, petite, graceful
- Reddish hair
- Clever
- Manipulator
- Charming
- A liar
- Dishonest
- False, shady
- Somebody who tells you what you want to hear and then goes behind your back
- In a health context, it can represent the doctor or a specialist
- A detective, police officer

HEALTH AND BODY PART:

- Could be something wrong
- Something needs investigation
- A misdiagnosis

- It can suggest to get a second opinion
- The senses: nose, eyes, ears
- Sometimes, it comes up as sinus

MONEY:

- Be aware of scammers
- Fraud
- It's risky
- Depending on the context and question, it can also mean that money is coming in through work and hustling

ADVICE:

- Use your cleverness to influence a situation to your advantage
- Use your quick-witted mind to get what you want but in a positive way
- Be strategic
- Be street smart, be skillful

OBJECTS:

- A trap

TIMING:

- 2 weeks

IN A GRAND TABLEAU, IF THE FOX CARD IS VERY CLOSE OR CLOSE TO THE SIGNIFICATOR CARD:

Having the Fox very close or close to the Significator is a warning. The Significator should be very aware of his/her surroundings, especially the people in one's life. There might be manipulation involved. Always check if the Fox is touching any Life Area cards. This way, you get an idea of where the falseness is coming from and in which Life Areas to be careful.

IN A GRAND TABLEAU, IF THE FOX IS FAR OR VERY FAR FROM THE SIGNIFICATOR:

Having the Fox far or very far from the Significator is a positive sign. In these positions, the Fox cannot harm the Man/Woman. But check which cards are affected by the Fox. In a Grand Tableau, look which card is next to the Fox; check where the Fox's nose is pointing. It shows where the wrongness is coming from.

Example Questions and Interpretations:

- Will I get the job?

Letter + Fox + Key = Yes, the job is yours.

- Will I get the job promotion?

Crossroads + Fox + Coffin = No, unfortunately not. It could be a termination.

- Is it safe to sign these documents?

Scythe + Fox + Letter = No, pay attention; something is wrong. Fraud.

- Is this friendship good for me?

Mice + Fox + Dog = No, it's a false friendship, a manipulative friend.

- What can you tell me about this financial transaction?

Fox + Fish + Coffin = financial fraud, leads to bankruptcy.

Chapter Nineteen

Card #15 - Bear - 10 of Clubs

Jealousy is when you count someone else's blessings instead of your own.

- Roy T. Bennett -

The Bear card #15 is a **neutral** card, but it can turn **positive** when surrounded by positive cards and **negative** when surrounded by negative cards.

- The core meaning of the Bear card is **good fortune,** but with it might come envy and jealousy

- In French cartomancy, the 10 of clubs is associated with money; that's why I use it as my finance card.

- The Bear talks about prosperity, power, strength, protection

- Stability

- Help is coming

- Support

- Security

- Surrounded by negative cards, it brings out the negative sides of the Bear, like envy and jealousy

- Overprotection

- Authority

- The Bear also stands for finances and diet

- In a money reading surrounded by positive cards, it can be a large amount of money

- For me, the Bear very often shows up as a Boss, a manager in a high position

IN A RELATIONSHIP:

- The Bear describes a strong and stable relationship, but with negative cards, it shows that the partner is overprotective and dominant; the partner might be controlling and jealous. It can also be bullying.

- It's a nourishing relationship

- The relationship is solid and secure

DESCRIBING A PERSON:

- It's a strong person

- Big and heavy

- Lots of hair

- Can be overweight

- A bodybuilder

- A boss, a manager in a high position

- Authority figure

- Can represent a protective mother

- With positive cards, the Bear is very caring and nurturing

- With negative cards, the Bear is aggressive

- A person who has courage

HEALTH AND BODY PART:

- The Bear represents diet and nutrition

- Keep track of what you eat

- Obesity

- Anything that has to do with weight management

- With negative cards around can indicate eating disorders

- Stomach

- The hair and hair growth

MONEY:

- Abundance

- Prosperity

- A large amount of money

- Financial security

- A lucrative investment

- In a financial reading, when I get Bear + Ship + Clover = A money transfer from overseas.

ADVICE:

- Use your strength

- Be fearless

- Show your authority

- Protect

- Be caring

- Eat

OBJECTS:

- Anything that has to do with food, for example, a restaurant

- Anything that has to do with money

TIMING:

- 2 weeks

- Between 6-8 months

IN A GRAND TABLEAU, I look at the card underneath the Bear (where the paws are pointing), which gives me a clue about where the envy is coming from and I look at which cards are surrounding the Bear, to get an idea of how my client's finances are.

IN A GRAND TABLEAU, IF THE BEAR IS VERY CLOSE OR CLOSE TO THE SIGNIFICATOR:

The closer the Bear, the stronger the Significator is. The Bear brings prosperity and good fortune, but watch out if the Bear is surrounded by negative cards - it comes with jealousy and envy. Pay attention to who your friends are and what information you share with them. What subject the Bear represents in one's life depends on the context and the question. Check what cards are around the Bear card. Before I do a reading, I ask my client about all the people in his/her life so I know how to activate/charge the Bear card. That way, I know if the Bear represents a person (a boss, a mother, etc.) or is talking about finances. It's good to have the Bear close but together with positive cards.

IN A GRAND TABLEAU, IF THE BEAR IS FAR OR VERY FAR FROM THE SIGNIFICATOR:

In these positions, the Bear does not bring prosperity. If the Bear falls far, then be careful who your friends are! As I mentioned before, look at which card lies underneath the Bear; the card under the Bear is from where the envy is coming. Also, check if there are any Life Area cards around the Bear that are influenced by the Bear.

Client Example:

Lydia asked me: "Will my financial situation improve within the next 3 months?" I pulled:

Clover + Mice + Bear + Cross =

Unfortunately, no, not within the next three months. Having the Cross as the last card shows a big financial burden. It would be a little better to have the Clover card as the last card. Then, we can say there is a positive improvement, see the example below:

Letter + Bear + Stork + Sun + Clover = This card combination was a letter from a boss that brought a successful change and big luck.

CHAPTER TWENTY

CARD #16 - STARS - 6 OF HEARTS

*To make a wish on a shooting star
you must first believe it can come true!*

The Stars card #16 is a **positive** card unless negative cards are following the Stars. Unfortunately, if negative cards surround the Stars, misfortune will follow, especially if the dark side of the Clouds is touching the Stars. This announces unhappy circumstances that may last a while. Positive cards around the Stars are a good omen. The Stars expand the positivity of the positive cards around them, so a miracle can be expected. If the Stars are the last card in a line reading (for example, a line of 5), positive and successful outcomes will materialize. They give hope and harmony - it's the light at the end of the tunnel.

- The core meaning of the Stars is **LUCK**
- Hope or ambition of achieving something
- The stars can also represent one's intentions
- The Stars show you the direction
- The Stars give you guidance
- The Stars show you that you are on the right path
- The Stars also represent networking, GPS, and maps
- Together with the Child card, it could indicate a new path
- Happiness and progress
- The Stars are associated with plenty, many, vast, a spread of
- Something is taking shape
- Wishes

IN A RELATIONSHIP:

- Depending on the cards that surround the Stars, **this relationship is serious, heartfelt,** and sincere
- It's true love
- Falling in love
- A romantic date

DESCRIBING A PERSON:

- Could have acne, skin marks, freckles, birthmarks

- Very appealing, beautiful eyes

- Somebody who is hopeful and confident about the future

- An optimist

- A popular person

- A dreamy person

- Somebody who's guiding others

- A consultant

- Advisor

HEALTH AND BODY PART:

- The skin

- In a health context, it can be skin rashes – eczema, acne, skin fungus, etc.

- It can also talk about sleeplessness, for example, Stars + Mice; the Mice card stands for worries and anxiety, which causes insomnia

- Depending on the question, in a health context, it indicates recovery and gives hope for a positive outcome. But if you, for example, describe specifically a cancer disease, then it indicates the spreading of the cancer. How you formulate the question is very important in the Lenormand.

MONEY:

- Money flows into one's life through some form of recognition

- All is well with the finances

ADVICE:

- Dream big

- Visualize your goals

- Believe
- Be hopeful
- Have faith
- Make a plan

OBJECTS:

- The stars in the sky
- A map
- GPS
- Internet
- Electricity
- Astrology
- Gemstones
- Anything that looks like a star

TIMING:

- Around 2 weeks
- At nighttime

IN A GRAND TABLEAU, IF THE STARS ARE VERY CLOSE OR CLOSE TO THE SIGNIFICATOR CARD:

Having the Stars very close or close and surrounded by positive cards indicates success in one's efforts to achieve something. Your plans are going in the right direction, and you are on the right path. Also, it is best to have the Stars card above the Significator card rather than below. That way, the Stars will shine down on the Significator card and give him/her clarity.

IN A GRAND TABLEAU, IF THE STARS ARE FAR OR VERY FAR FROM THE SIGNIFICATOR:

Having the Stars far or very far from the Significator indicates that success, clarity, and reaching one's goals are, at the moment, out of reach. But check which cards surround the Stars, especially which Life Area cards are influenced by the Stars, and see if there are any negative cards around the Stars.

Client Examples:

My client Jane wanted to find out what was causing her acne. While shuffling the cards, I activated the Tree card to represent Jane's health. Then, when I was done shuffling, I looked through the cards where the Tree card was, and I pulled the card that came before the Tree and the card that came after the Tree. This is what I got:

Moon + Tree + Stars

Since this is a health context, the Moon is talking about hormones, and the Tree is our Focus Card and represents Jane's health. The last card is the Stars, which affirms Jane's question; the Stars stand for acne. The answer was very simple: Jane's acne is caused by hormones.

A couple of weeks later, Jane went to see a dermatologist and a hormonal imbalance was confirmed.

PLEASE NOTE:

It takes years of experience and lots of practice to read about health and make a health prediction. Please always refer the client to a qualified medical professional. Card readers are not doctors! But we can give them advice and peace of mind or prepare them for what could be expected.

Next, I'll share a story that is very dear to me. My client Magdalena wanted to know if her son Adam was still alive because she hadn't heard from him for many weeks. He had to go to war in Syria. I shuffled the cards and pulled:

Snake + Scythe + Child + Stars + Key + Letter

The first card is the Snake, which stands for problems and complications, but the Scythe is cutting those problems and complications away/is clearing them. After the Scythe card, we have the child, which stands for something new/a new beginning but can also indicate a get-together and joy. The Stars + Key at the end of this line shows us a big yes - her son is still alive, and she's going to hear from him very soon! The Stars card talks about hope and faith. In combination with the Key, it's a very powerful combination. It brings solutions and recognition and can also stand for an award. Also, in a love/relationship context, it's a very auspicious constellation.

Outcome: A couple of months later, my client Magdalena told me her son Adam had finally contacted her.

I love it when I can give my clients peace of mind and hope in stressful situations!

Personal example:

Some time ago, I suddenly lost my internet connection. It was very strange, and I had no clue what had happened. So I asked the cards: "What happened to my internet connection?" I pulled:

Ship + Snake + Scythe + Stars + Mountain

The Ship in this reading represents my automatic vacuum robot. The Ship is the only card that has an engine. This little vacuum cleaner went over the cables (Snake) and pulled them out / cut the connection (Scythe) to the power outlet, and that caused the issue of having no internet (Mountain). The Lenormand can be very literal at times and incredibly helpful!

Chapter Twenty-One

Card #17 - Stork - Queen of Hearts

*Progress is impossible without change,
and those who cannot change their minds
cannot change anything.*
- George Bernard Shaw -

The Stork card #17 is a **positive** card that talks about improvements. But if a negative card follows the Stork, the improvement is blocked or delayed. For example, if you get Stork + Mountain, obstacles are in the way. On the other hand, if you get

Mountain + Stork, that means you are overcoming those obstacles.

As I mentioned before, I use directional reading. In other words, I look where the Stork is flying towards. This depends on what Lenormand deck you are using; every deck has different Storks that fly either to the right or to the left - so you have to adjust accordingly. I prefer the Stork flying towards the right side because I read the cards from left to right.

- The core meaning of the Stork is **change**. The Stork announces a change for the better or worse.

- It symbolizes progress, a promotion, an upgrade

- It can also indicate leaving or moving on; it all depends on the question and the context. In my readings, I always want to see where the Stork is flying to, so I draw a clarifying card for confirmation.

- The Stork, together with the Ship card, can indicate air travel

- Together with the House card, it announces a move, a change of residence, or just a renovation. The surrounding cards are important to interpret the Stork; they will give you information about what kind of change it is.

IN A RELATIONSHIP:

- In a relationship context, the Stork is announcing a change in the relationship - what kind of change is described by the surrounding cards and especially the card that follows after the Stork.

- An improvement in the relationship

- Moving forward, progressing

- If the Stork lands as the last card in a line reading, that could indicate leaving or moving on. That's why when I have the Stork in this position, I always draw a clarifying card to see where the Stork is flying to. For example, if the Ring card appears after the Stork (Stork + Ring), that could mean moving in together - the Stork is flying towards a commitment. However, if I get a negative card like the Scythe comes after the Stork, it could indicate a separation or a definite ending.

DESCRIBING A PERSON:

- When I get the Stork to describe somebody, it's an elegant and graceful person

- Slim

- Tall with long legs

- Could be a dancer

- Likes to change one's environment, is moving around

- Always looking for a better place or situation

- Wanting to improve and progress

- A productive person

HEALTH AND BODY PART:

- Legs

- Recovery

- Things are getting better

- In a health context, it stands for recovery or fertility.

- The Stork announces a pregnancy, especially if the Child, Moon, Anchor, Tree, and Garden card are around. If the Bird card is touching the Stork, it could indicate a pregnancy in the early stages (the first 3 months), and Stork and Child talk about a pregnancy in later stages.

MONEY:

- More money is coming in through a promotion or a raise in salary

- A change for the better

- An improvement

ADVICE:

- Move on

- Change is good

- Improve

- Expect more and better

- Be a perfectionist

OBJECTS:

- Anything that has to do with children, for example, a kindergarten

- Or a place that is high up, for example, a wardrobe

TIMING:

- It will happen when the seasons are changing, for example, spring to summer, or fall to winter, or winter to spring (because the Stork is a migrating bird; they migrate in the winter and return in the spring)

- Around 2 weeks

A popular question in a reading is: "Will he come back to me?" **IN A GRAND TABLEAU, IF** the Stork card connects to the Man, then I can say yes, he will come back to you.

IN A GRAND TABLEAU, IF THE STORK IS VERY CLOSE OR CLOSE TO THE SIGNIFICATOR CARD:

If the Stork is in the comfort zone of the Significator (in other words, very close or close), that means there will be a change in one's life. The kind of change that will occur is explained by the cards that touch and surround the Stork card. Check which Life Area cards are close by. For example, if you have the Stork + House combination nearby, that indicates moving house. The closer the Stork, the sooner the change will occur.

When I do a Grand Tableau, I always look first at the very last column on the right side (the very last row from top to bottom). If I see that the Stork lands there, that means there will be a very significant change in the Significator's life. What kind of change will be explained by the surrounding cards. If the Stork lands in the very first column on the left side, that means the Significator has already gone through a transformation.

IN A GRAND TABLEAU, IF THE STORK IS FAR OR VERY FAR FROM THE SIGNIFICATOR:

That means the Significator still has to wait for the change to happen. See what Life Area cards the Stork is touching. Usually, my clients ask me to do a Grand Tableau for 6 months.

This is how I calculate the timing in a Grand Tableau:

- 2 columns are a month and a half
- 4 columns are 3 months
- 6 columns are 4.5 month
- 8 columns are 6 months

Then, I look where the Significator landed, and from the Man/Woman card, I count the columns to the Stork. That gives me an approximate timeframe for when the change will occur.

Client Examples:

Robert asked: Where will my new project at work lead to? I pulled:

Mice + Clouds + Key + Stork + Moon

My answer: At first, there will be worries (Mice) and confusion (Clouds), but solutions will be found (Key). It will progress (Stork) and lead to recognition (Moon).

Maria asked me: "Will I be able to move by the spring?" I pulled:

Crossroads + House + Stork + Mountain

My answer: No, your move will be delayed (Mountain).

After this reading, she asked me: "Why will there be a delay?" I pulled:

Mice + Child + Whip + Fish + Mountain

My answer: The delay (Mountain) has to do with her children (Child card) and her finances (Fish), and Whip + Fish = hard times with money and financial difficulties.

6 months later, Maria gave me feedback: Maria's move was indeed delayed because of other unexpected expenses she had because of her children.

Chapter Twenty-Two

Card #18 - Dog - 10 of Hearts

True friends are never apart,
Maybe in distance but never in heart.

The Dog card #18 is a **positive** card, **BUT** the Dog is highly influenced by the surrounding cards! Negative cards can turn the Dog into a negative card; in that case, you must watch your back!!

- The core meaning of the Dog is **loyalty**

- You can always depend on a good Dog
- A Dog can guide, protect, and watch over you
- It gives security
- The Dog symbolizes faithfulness
- The Dog represents a friend you can trust
- The Dog could represent a partner or a 3rd party
- In health readings, the Dog shows up as a doctor
- The Dog card can represent your pet

IN A RELATIONSHIP:

- It is a trustworthy relationship
- A safe relationship
- This relationship is based on true friendship
- In combination with the Tree card, it talks about a soulmate and a very strong relationship
- Your best friend as your partner
- Loyal and committed

DESCRIBING A PERSON:

- A true friend
- A reliable friend who is always there to help
- Somebody who helps you when you are in need
- A friend you can trust
- A protector

- A very loving and loyal friend
- Faithful

HEALTH AND BODY PART:

- Nose and sinus
- Tongue
- Sometimes, the Dog card came up as one's immune system
- In health readings, the Dog shows up as the doctor, a specialist, or a counselor

MONEY:

- Money will come in through the help of a friend
- Unemployment benefits, financial aid
- The financial situation is stable

ADVICE:

- Be there for others
- Be protective
- Be loyal
- Be a friend to someone by offering help or support
- Be friendly, generous, and considerate

OBJECTS:

- Anything that has to do with security, for example, a monitor, detector, recorder, security camera, etc.
- Your pet
- Anything that looks like a Dog, for example, a stuffed animal

TIMING:

- 18 days, the 18th of the month

IN A GRAND TABLEAU, IF THE DOG IS VERY CLOSE OR CLOSE TO THE SIGNIFICATOR CARD:

In these positions, the Significator can count on unconditional and sincere friendships. Good people are around. Help and support are within reach. When the Dog is close but is surrounded by negative cards, it could be a friend in trouble. The Dog can be a best friend from your surroundings, or it could be your brother, sister, or any other family member.

The Dog can also represent a guardian angel. To get a specific message from a guardian angel I look at which cards are surrounding the Dog. The Dog symbolizes friendship, so look at which cards are around the Dog to see what's going on.

IN A GRAND TABLEAU, IF THE DOG IS FAR OR VERY FAR FROM THE SIGNIFICATOR:

In these positions, the Dog is too far to protect or warn you. If the Dog is far away and surrounded by negative cards, you should be careful about whom you call a friend. Especially if the clouds are next to the Dog, it can mean untrustworthy friends or people who act as one's friends.

Client Examples:

Jason had an argument with his best friend, and the friendship was over.

Jason asked: "Will there be a chance of healing this friendship?" I pulled:

Whip + Dog + Coffin + Lilies + Sun + Anchor

My answer: Yes, there will be a reconciliation, but it will take some time (Lilies). The Whip shows the argument with the friend (Whip + Dog), and the Dog + Coffin shows the end of the friendship.

The Lilies card tells me it will take some time, but in the end, there will be reconciliation, and this friendship will last, as shown by the Anchor.

Often, in my readings, people ask me about a friendship and whether it is really a sincere friend or not... Now, if I get card combinations like Fox + Dog, Snake + Dog, and Clouds + Dog, then one should be really careful whom you call a friend. These could be people who will betray you.

There is a saying: True friends, you can count on one hand!

Chapter Twenty-Three

Card #19 - Tower - 6 of Spades

A lack of boundaries
Invites a lack of respect.

The Tower card #19 is a **neutral** card. It can turn positive if surrounded by positive cards and negative when surrounded by negative cards.

- The core meaning of the Tower card is **longevity**

- If it's near the Man/Woman card, it symbolizes a long, happy life (if surrounded by positive cards), but if it's far from the Man/Woman card, it could indicate an illness, especially if the Clouds card is touching the Tower with its dark side.

- The Tower is one of the health cards (Health cards: Tree, Coffin, Whip, Tower, Clouds)

- The Tower symbolizes one's life

- It talks about institutions, like a big firm or company

- All legal matters are associated with the Tower

- Restrictions and boundaries

- Rules and regulations

- Anything that has to do with legal matters and official institutions

- The government

- The law

- Airports, schools, hospitals, higher education

- Depending on the context, it can stand for isolation and loneliness

- Ambitions

- The Tower can also refer to the past

- **All depends on the context, the question, and the surrounding cards.** The Tower can mean protection, or in a negative sense, it can be confinement.

- The Tower can also represent your ambitions, goals, purpose, and a strong desire for advancement

PLEASE NOTE:

The Tower card in the Lenormand system has nothing to do with the Tower card in the Tarot. It's not the same - this card has a completely different meaning!

IN A RELATIONSHIP:

- This is a lifelong relationship: When a client asks me: "Will this relationship last?" If I get the Tower card, it will last a lifetime.

- The Tower can also mean that a relationship is now official

- It's a serious, stable, and secure relationship

    - But again, depending on the context, the question, and the surrounding cards, the Tower can describe one's feelings; for example, Tower + Heart = a lonely heart and

    - Tower + Ring = could be a divorce or a past marriage

- With negative cards, the relationship is cold and lonely.

DESCRIBING A PERSON:

- A tall, slim person, could have a flat chest

- Grey hair

- It can be a person who has high ambitions

- Somebody with a high level of education

- Someone who aims to reach high goals

- Somebody who has achieved success through one's efforts

- Someone who has high standards

- High self-esteem

- A lonely person, a loner

- A lawyer

- Attorney

- A judge

- A court clerk

HEALTH AND BODY PART:

- The Tower stands for one's life expectancy and old age
- The spine, the back
- The Tower represents all health-related institutions like a hospital
- Depending on other card combinations, the Tower, in a health context, can also talk about depression or mental illness

MONEY:

- Money is saved in the bank

ADVICE:

- Create some boundaries
- Raise your spirit
- Uplift
- Be organized
- Arrange according to a specific plan - be structured
- Move from a lower to a higher place or position

OBJECTS:

- A tall apartment building
- A Tower
- A wardrobe
- Anything that is tall

TIMING:

- From 19 days to 4-5 months

IN A GRAND TABLEAU, IF THE TOWER CARD IS VERY CLOSE OR CLOSE TO THE SIGNIFICATOR:

It is always very favorable to have the Tower card as close as possible to the Significator because it indicates that the Man/Woman will reach his/her goals. It symbolizes a happy and long life. The Significator will reach a high age. The Tower represents one's life. The cards that surround the Tower will give information on how the quality of one's life will be for the duration of this Grand Tableau. It is always good to have the Tower close and surrounded by positive cards and to have the Clouds card as far away as possible. If the Clouds card is touching the Tower with its dark side, that is a very negative constellation and can indicate illness and even death - It all depends on the other card constellations.

IN A GRAND TABLEAU, IF THE TOWER CARD IS FAR OR VERY FAR FROM THE SIGNIFICATOR:

In these positions, the Significator does not have much control over reaching his/her goals, and it indicates that the lifespan of the Significator is not very long. In that case, hopefully, the Tower in these positions is surrounded by positive cards. Having positive cards around the Tower indicates a secure and stable foundation. Surrounded by negative cards, it brings out the negative attributes of the Tower card.

Card Combination Examples:

Whip + Tower = Can be a court case or troubles with the authorities

Tower + Whip = Could be a prison

Tower + Key = Can talk about a liberation or a successful legal case

Client Example:

I did this reading for a friend of mine. My friend Lily wanted to know what to expect from her brother, whom she hadn't seen in a while. Their relationship was always very difficult. I pulled:

Ship + Whip + Tower + Mice + Mountain

This line doesn't look very promising. Here, we can see how the Tower can turn into a negative card when surrounded by negative cards. The Ship indicates a change and shows us where the energy is flowing.

Whip + Tower= Shows an argument between Lily and her brother

Tower + Mice= Stressful orders from the brother

Mice + Mountain = Left my friend Lily feeling very frustrated, stressed, and trapped.

A couple of weeks later, Lily told me that her brother wanted to get more of the inheritance, which was split between both. He threatened to go to court.

Personal Example:

A personal sad story from me about the Tower + Clouds combination:

About a month and a half before my mother transitioned, I had a bad feeling about her health. At the same time, I was getting ready to go on a trip the following month. I was very excited and curious about how my trip was going to play out. So, I did a Box spread for myself. In the spread, I got:

Ship + Scythe combination with other negative cards like Mice and Cross.

Whenever I get the Ship + Scythe combination regarding a trip, it indicates a canceled trip. I was very surprised and didn't understand why the cards showed me that my journey would be canceled. I was disappointed, so I did another reading asking why I wouldn't go on this trip. I had my ticket already, and everything was set.

What the cards showed me was not pleasant at all. I knew it had to do with my mother's health. The Tower + Clouds combination showed up together with the Tree card as the focus card. The other health cards showed up, too (Whip + Coffin), and the Scythe and the Cross card were there. Basically, all the negative cards were in one spread. When I saw these negative constellations, I knew something bad would happen.

A couple of days later, I did a Box spread again, but this time specifically for my mother's health...what shocked me exactly the same cards showed up. Then I knew she would be passing away, and that's why my trip would be canceled. A month and a half later, my mother's condition became worse, and 5 days later, she passed away. I rather say she transitioned into another dimension. Energy never dies.

Numerous times I used my cards to communicate with my mother. For example, if I was looking for certain documents, I had to find them after her death... She guided me through my cards to find them. I am very grateful to understand what the Lenormand cards want to convey.

Chapter Twenty-Four

CARD #20 - GARDEN- 8 OF SPADES

The greatest gift of the garden is the restoration of the five senses.

-Hanna Rion-

The Garden card #20 is a **neutral** card. Together with positive cards, the Garden turns positive, but surrounded by negative cards, the Garden turns negative.

- The core meaning of the Garden is **good company**

- The Garden has to do with people, a group of people, or just communicating with one's close friends

- It is any type of gathering, such as a get-together, party, birthday, wedding, funeral, event, meeting, seminar, demonstration, etc., any social place where many people meet. The surrounding cards will give more information about what it exactly is.

- Depending on the context, the Garden can also represent networking

- The Garden represents beauty, harmony, relaxation, nature, feeling good, peaceful, and contentment - a feeling of happiness and satisfaction. Think about how you feel when you are sitting in a beautiful garden.

IN A RELATIONSHIP:

This is a tricky card, and many readers interpret it incorrectly. How to interpret the Garden correctly **really depends on the context, the question, and the surrounding cards.**

- It can indicate meeting new people

- Going out and dating several people at the same time

- It could mean having several sexual relationships without committing to anyone

- It can also advise you to go out more and socialize

- When I get this card for a couple then, I always draw clarifying cards to explain the situation more

- The Garden is one of the Tree cards (Tree, House, Crossroads, Child). If all Tree cards are together, it symbolizes the accomplishment of one's wishes and a bright future!

- It can also be a positive card in a relationship reading; it can mean that the relationship is flourishing and blossoming. But, as I explained before, I have to look at the whole picture and the other card combinations. Don't make a judgment with just one or two cards!

DESCRIBING A PERSON:

- A beautiful person
- Very attractive
- Elegant
- A person who likes nature
- A very social person
- Somebody who likes to go out and party
- Likes to communicate
- An outgoing person
- Inspired
- Expressive
- Creative

HEALTH AND BODY PART:

- The immune system
- Contagious infections
- A pandemic
- Fertility, if Child + Stork is near and also Tree and Anchor, then it could indicate a pregnancy.
- In a health reading, having the Garden next to the Tree can indicate getting support from your close friends

MONEY:

- Prosperity and abundance

- Money flows in through a successful enterprise
- Social security
- Unemployment insurance
- Medicare

ADVICE:

- Make new friends
- Socialize
- Be more outgoing
- Network
- Involve your connections
- Communicate

OBJECTS:

- Any public place where people gather
- A garden, a park
- A network

TIMING:

- 20 days
- The 20th of the month
- Sometimes, it comes up as springtime

IN A GRAND TABLEAU, IF THE GARDEN IS VERY CLOSE OR CLOSE TO THE SIGNIFICATOR CARD:

To have the Garden in these positions means that the Significator will be respected by his/her friends. There are good people around the Significator. Support and loyalty will be there. It can also be said that the Significator is socializing. Always check which cards are surrounding the Garden card. This will give you information about what kind of people are around the Man/Woman card and from what Life Area. For example, if the work card is touching the Garden, it talks about one's work colleagues. It is always good to have the Garden close by and surrounded by positive cards that bring out the positive aspects of the Garden card.

IN A GRAND TABLEAU, IF THE GARDEN CARD IS FAR OR VERY FAR FROM THE SIGNIFICATOR:

The Garden card in these positions is a warning sign. Be alarmed about false friendships and be careful who your friends are. There are people who are just pretending to be a friend; there are people around who put on a false appearance. Support and loyalty are out of reach. During hard times, we see who our true friends are. Check if there are any negative cards and people cards around the Garden that will show you where the disloyalty is coming from. It also indicates that the Significator is not very social at the moment.

Card Combination Example:

Garden + Tower = This friendship is one for life

Client Examples:

Question: Why is he not calling me?

Heart + Book + Rider + Garden

Answer: Because he is secretly going out to see other people

This was a daily draw I get very frequently, and I am always happy to see this combination:

Ship + Lilies + Garden + Child + Birds =

Long distance (Ship) communications (Birds) with close friends (Garden) which were very joyful (Child) and satisfying (Lilies).

Question: How will my meeting go?

Garden + Scythe

Answer: The meeting will be canceled.

Chapter Twenty-Five

Card #21 - Mountain - 8 of Clubs

Temporary setbacks are
Overshadowed by persistence.
- Quentin L. Cook -

The Mountain card #21 is a **negative** card.

- The core meaning of the Mountain card is an **obstacle** and an **enemy**

- The Mountain talks about obstacles, delays, postponements, setbacks, and problems

- Heavy burdens (especially with the Cross combination)

- A blockage - something is blocking your progress

- A standstill

- Resistance

- Isolation

- Nasty cold people

- The Mountain brings a heavy atmosphere to the reading, but don't be discouraged; there is always a way around the Mountain!

- Depending on the context and question, the Mountain can also be a good thing - it talks about staying, not moving.

  - For example:

  - Will I lose my job? And you get the Mountain followed by the Anchor or Tree card, which means no, you are staying where you are. I get these card combinations frequently when I'm doing readings for my clients. So, I know the Mountain is not always bad - it all depends on one's situation and the question.

- The Mountain is a timing card; it symbolizes that there will be delays and that something will take a long time

IN A RELATIONSHIP:

- Things aren't moving forward

- It's usually characterized by a lack of communication or a feeling that you don't have fun anymore

- in a relationship reading, if the question is: Is he/she leaving me? The answer would be no; he/she is not going anywhere.

- The partner is detached, disinterested

- Not showing of feeling interest

- A cold relationship

- Disharmony

- But again, I can't stress enough about the importance of the context and the question! Here is an example:

  - If you ask, "Is this relationship a serious one?" And if you get Mountain + Ring + Sun, then the answer would be yes; it is a very solid, strong relationship.

  - Another example: "Is he leaving me for good?" If you get Mountain + Anchor or Mountain + Tree, that means NO, he is not going anywhere!

DESCRIBING A PERSON:

- A big and strong person

- Can have a large head, baldness, or grey hair

- A stubborn person

- Cold, not friendly

- Unpleasant

- Aloof

- Commanding

- Lonely

- Doesn't show emotions

- Unsentimental

- Headstrong

HEALTH AND BODY PART:

- The head
- The breasts
- Staying in bed
- Unable to move
- A blockage
- Constipation
- A swelling
- A tumor
- Arthritis
- Stiffness

MONEY:

- Financial obstacles
- Hard times with money
- Debts

ADVICE:

- Don't change your opinion or give in to an argument
- Stay with your beliefs - don't change anything
- Be strong-willed
- Stay where you are

- Don't give up, and keep moving forward

OBJECTS:

- Mountains
- A hill
- Stones
- An isolated place far away from town

TIMING:

- 21 days, 3 weeks, 3 months
- The 21st of the month
- It takes a long time
- Winter time

IN A GRAND TABLEAU, IF THE MOUNTAIN CARD IS VERY CLOSE OR CLOSE TO THE SIGNIFICATOR CARD:

In these positions, the Significator has to deal with an obstacle or an enemy. The cards surrounding the Mountain will explain how severe it is. Check if the Mountain card is touching any Life Area cards (for example, Work (Fox or Market Card) or family (House Card)) and see if there are any other people next to the Mountain. Then, you will know who the enemy might be and from where the obstacle is coming.

It is always very interesting to see which card lies under the Mountain! Imagine what pressure the card that is under the Mountain has to endure. For example, if the Man/Woman card is under the Mountain, that means he/she has a heavy burden over their head; he/she is dealing with lots of problems. The Mountain makes everything heavy and difficult.

But if the Mountain is under the Significator card, it will be much easier to overcome the obstacle; the Significator has more control over the challenges. Another example is if you have the Ring card under the Mountain, that means the relationship is affected by obstacles; the heavy weight of the Mountain is pressing down on the relationship (Ring).

Also, check on which side the Mountain is. To the left means in the past, and to the right means that the obstacle is still coming (future). Negative cards make the Mountain more negative, and positive cards make the obstacles of the Mountain smaller and easier to deal with.

IN A GRAND TABLEAU, IF THE MOUNTAIN CARD IS FAR OR VERY FAR FROM THE SIGNIFICATOR:

In these positions, the Significator is saved from obstacles. The traditional Lenormand instructions state that if the Mountain is far, you can count on protection from very powerful and strong friends, but this is the case if the Dog, the Garden, and the Child card are close or very close to the Significator for support. There will be help from friends in a time of need. Check which cards (especially Life Area cards) get affected by the Mountain card.

Card Combination Examples:

- Stork + Mountain = Obstacles are in the way
- Mountain + Stork = Successfully overcoming an obstacle
- Mountain + Scythe = Obstacles are cleared away.
- Mountain + Ship = This can either be a delayed trip or a canceled trip (the surrounding cards will give more info).

Client Examples:

Question: "Will I be able to visit my boyfriend this weekend?"

Fish + Mountain + Tree =

Answer: No, you are not going anywhere. The Mountain card indicates staying, not going anywhere.

Question: "Will my troubles go away soon?"

Mountain + Cross + Incense burner (Card #38) + Key =

Answer: The Mountain and the Cross symbolize burdens, trouble, and worries. I always love to see the Incense burner after a set of heavy cards because the obstacles will be cleared away. The Key, in the end, shows us that solutions will be found.

Question: Linda asked me: "Will I get the new job?"

Letter + Mountain + Sun =

Answer: Yes, you will get the job. But the job offer (Letter) will be delayed. I pulled a clarifying card to make sure, and I got the Anchor, which means reaching one's goals.

A couple of weeks later, Linda gave me feedback, and yes, she got the job, but there were some delays with the paperwork.

Personal Example:

This was one of my daily draws:

Ship + Scythe + Mountain =

I did this daily to see if I would be satisfied with a package. I ordered a French press coffee maker made of glass. When I saw this line, I knew something would be wrong… It turned out that my Shipment (Ship) arrived broken (Scythe). The Mountain here represents the glass. My experience over the years shows that Scythe + Mountain means either cutting through obstacles or breaking things into small pieces. Sometimes, the cards are very literal!

CHAPTER TWENTY-SIX

CARD #22 - CROSSROADS - QUEEN OF DIAMONDS

Sometimes it's the smallest decisions
That can change your life forever.
- Keri Russell -

The Crossroads card #22 is a **neutral** card. It is influenced by the surrounding cards.

• The core meaning of the Crossroads, according to traditional instructions, is **challenging decisions.** I don't quite agree with the challenging part - **for me,**

it depends on the context, the question, and the cards that surround and follow the Crossroads. If the Crossroads are surrounded by positive cards, that means the outcome will be joyful, pleasant, and very satisfying. It's not the Crossroads that is bad... it's the cards that touch the Crossroads that influence and color it - either negative or positive.

- It's time to make a decision

- The Crossroads can mean going separate ways

- Having multiple choices

- It can stand for multiple things or people

- Alternatives, options

- A way out

- A turning point

- Things can turn out a different way than planned; the surrounding cards will explain what and why

- It can show where the direction is going...**if I have the Crossroads as the last card in a line reading, I always pull a clarifying card because I want to see where the Crossroad is leading to or ending with.**

- In daily draws, it can just stand for a road

- It can stand for the journey you are taking and where it goes

- This card has to do with free will! You are the one who makes the decision; after you make the decision, the cards will show you where your decision leads.

- It can also indicate a double life and cheating

- If the Crossroad is landing on the left or right side of the Significator card, that is a sign of unfaithfulness, but I always clarify with a separate reading to make sure.

- Now, the Clouds touching the Crossroads (especially with its dark side) is a very negative constellation. It is a sign of misfortune; troubles and unhappiness are on the horizon.

IN A RELATIONSHIP:

- It can mean a separation
- One of the partners is not being faithful
- Multiple sexual partners
- A double life
- Don't want to commit
- Doubts and uncertainty about where the relationship is going

DESCRIBING A PERSON:

- Bisexuality (when the Crossroads is next to the Significator card and another third-party card is touching the Significator and the Crossroads, that's a red flag)
- A person who is always on the go and all over the place
- Wishy-washy personality
- Hesitating
- Doubtful
- Undecided
- Nothing makes sense what this person is talking about
- A person with a double life
- Somebody who is disloyal
- This person could have two colored hair or highlights

HEALTH AND BODY PART:

- Arteries and veins
- The lymphatic system
- Can be advised to get a second opinion
- It can show medical options

NOTE:

THE CROSSROADS IS ONE OF THE TREE CARDS (**Tree cards**: Tree, House, Garden, Crossroads, and Child card). In a health context, it means that you still have options and a chance of recovery, no matter how bad the illness is. Of course, the surrounding cards will give more info. Hopefully, there are positive cards around the Crossroads.

MONEY:

- More than one source of income

ADVICE:

- It is time to make a decision
- Decide wisely! In a Grand Tableau, the card above and below the Crossroads will help you to make a decision

OBJECTS:

- A road
- A street
- An intersection
- An exit
- A fork
- Anything that has to do with decision-making

TIMING:

- 2 days, 2 weeks, 2 months
- The 22nd of a month

IN A GRAND TABLEAU, IF the Crossroads lands in the very last column of the Grand Tableau (the 8 column - right edge), it means that the Significator will go through a total change of direction...something in the Significator's life is going to change in a big way. The cards that surround the Crossroads will give information regarding what it will be. Also, if the Crossroads in that position is touched by ACTIVE CARDS like Rider, Ship, Birds, and Stork, it means that the decision will be made with absolute certainty. The timeframe depends on how far the Significator is from that 8 column.

IN A GRAND TABLEAU, IF THE CROSSROADS CARD IS VERY CLOSE OR CLOSE TO THE SIGNIFICATOR CARD:

If the Crossroads is touching the Significator card either on top or bottom or left or right, that means the Man/Woman has a decision to make. It shows the Significator has choices and options available. It might be a way out. The surrounding cards are very important when interpreting the Crossroads. Negative cards touching the Crossroads means there will be unpleasant difficulties on the journey. Especially negative cards like Clouds, Cross and Mice cause trouble.

IN A GRAND TABLEAU, IF THE CROSSROADS IS FAR OR VERY FAR FROM THE SIGNIFICATOR:

If the Crossroads is far away from the Significator, it means that the options and choices are, for the duration of this spread, difficult to reach or even out of reach. Check which cards, especially Life Area cards, are touching the Crossroads. It is always good to have positive cards around the Crossroads and the Clouds card as far as possible away from the Crossroads.

Card Combination Examples:

- Crossroads + Ship = Multiple trips
- Crossroads + Heart = Conflicting emotions

- Heart + Crossroads = Two lovers

- Ring + Crossroads = A separation, a double life. But I always do a bigger spread to confirm, or I pull clarifying cards to see what's coming after the Crossroads.

- Coffin + Crossroads = A new direction

- Scythe + Crossroads = A sudden decision

- Crossroads + Fish = Money coming in or a financial decision

- Crossroads + Letter = Multiple letters

- Crossroads + Scythe = Can be an accident on the road or a very decisive turn of events....the surrounding cards will give more information.

- Crossroads + Coffin = a negative decision or a negative turn

Client Example:

This story is about my client Brian, who came to me because of ongoing problems with his girlfriend. Brian wanted to know how things would be between them after an argument and a break-up. I pulled:

Whip + Ring + Crossroads + Heart + Stars

The Whip affirms the argument in this relationship.

Ring + Crossroads = This combination in a relationship context always tells us there are problems in this relationship. It could mean a separation, a double life, or going in circles.

The Crossroads + Heart combination in this scenario talks about conflicting emotions.

I love having the Heart + Stars at the end of this line reading because it shows that there is still hope for the couple to get back together, and they did for now...

Personal Example:

The cards can sometimes be very literal. This was a daily draw for me:

Line of 7: Rider + Woman + Crossroads + Coffin + Scythe + Clover + Spirit #37

That day, I went on a bike ride; I love riding my bike. The Rider here represents my bike, and the Woman card is me. While I was riding, I planned to go on a certain road, but when I got there, I saw it was closed because of construction (the Crossroads + Coffin = Dead-end), so I decided to go a different way. I was riding my bike, and all of a sudden, the front part of my bike became loose and totally detached (it's a folding bike). I almost caused an accident, but I was very lucky nothing happened to me on the street. People from the other side of the street witnessed this and told me I must have a guardian angel watching over me.

Coffin + Scythe = Accident

The Clover card shows my luck, and the Spirit card #37 is my guardian angel. I'll never forget this story.

Chapter Twenty-Seven
Card #23 - Mice - 7 of Clubs

What we have once enjoyed, we can never lose.
All that we love deeply becomes a part of us.

-Helen Keller-

The Mice card #23 is a **negative** card. Only in rare cases may it be neutral, for example, in an advice reading. The Mice card advises to be precise and exact - pay attention to detail. Depending on the context and question, the Mice card can refer to teamwork.

- The core meaning of the Mice card is **loss**
- Whenever I get the Mice card in a reading, it talks about stress, worries, anxiety, and loss
- Fears and doubts
- Nervousness and tension
- The feeling of something is nagging
- The lack of something
- Theft
- Something is becoming progressively worse
- Disappointments
- Things that gnaw away at you
- Damage
- Being concerned about something
- A small problem which is becoming bigger with time if it is not taken care of immediately

IN A RELATIONSHIP:

- Stresses and worries regarding your relationship
- A negative relationship that eats away at your heart
- An unstable and shaky connection
- Someone is trying to possess you
- This relationship is slowly deteriorating

- An uneasy, nervous relationship
- Love is getting less

DESCRIBING A PERSON:

- Thin hair
- Small teeth
- Petite body type
- Small/narrow looking face
- A stressed and worried person
- A person with anxiety
- A nervous and tense person
- A nail-biter
- A person who is hoarding
- A sick, fatigued person
- A person who is very difficult to please and likes only a small range of things - nit-picky
- Unpredictable
- Insecure
- A person with emotional baggage
- Penny-pinching - somebody who is very stingy with money
- Somebody who annoys people by constantly finding fault
- Someone who is unable to rest or relax

HEALTH AND BODY PART:

- Illness
- Bacterial infections
- Parasites
- Can be cancer (depending on the other card constellations)
- Stress and anxiety
- Nervous breakdown
- Something is eating away at your wellbeing
- The teeth
- Metabolism
- The nervous system
- Twitching
- Fatigue
- The health condition is declining

MONEY:

- Financial losses
- Theft
- Ruin
- Money goes out faster than it comes in

ADVICE:

- Let go, don't obsess
- Be pickier and pay attention to details

- Don't stress out, and don't worry
- The Mice card advises teamwork
- Examine and inspect closely and thoroughly
- Endure

OBJECTS:

- Any kind of pest
- A mouse
- Any little animal that looks like a mouse: rats, hamsters
- A crack, gap, or little hole

TIMING:

- Very fast
- Minutes, a few hours
- Less than a month
- The 23rd of the month

IN A GRAND TABLEAU, if the Significator is in the house of the Mice, that means the Man/Woman is very stressed and worried, may have anxiety, and may reject himself/herself.

IN A GRAND TABLEAU, IF THE MICE CARD IS VERY CLOSE OR CLOSE TO THE SIGNIFICATOR CARD:

Having the Mice card very close or close means the Significator will be a victim of a loss. Usually, we want all negative cards to fall as far as possible from the Significator, but the Mice card is the exception. Because if you have the Mice card close, there is a good chance of getting something back you have lost or was stolen. The exact meaning of what is lost or missing depends on the context and the cards that surround the Mice. Whatever the Mice stands for in a reading, it always causes anxiety and stress. Let's hope there are enough positive cards around to ease the negativity. If the Mice card is surrounded by more negative cards, that makes the impact of the Mice even worse.

IN A GRAND TABLEAU, IF THE MICE CARD IS FAR OR VERY FAR FROM THE SIGNIFICATOR CARD:

To have the Mice card far or very far from the Significator means that whatever is lost is lost for good. Check which cards (especially Life Area cards) are being influenced by the Mice.

Examples of Lost Items:

Mice in combination with:

- Bird card = lost cell phone
- Letter card = Lost documents, papers, or letters
- Book card = A lost book or misplaced magazines
- Ring card = Lost jewelry
- Fish card = Stolen money
- Rider card = A stolen bike or motorcycle
- Ship card = A stolen car
- Scythe card = Stolen or misplaced tools
- Bouquet card = Stolen paintings or any art piece
- House card = Can indicate a robbery (depending on other negative card constellations)
- Stars card = Stolen GPS device

Card Combination Examples:

I like to see a very positive card following the Mice card. This means in the end, all will be well. For example:

Mice + Key = A solution, a breakthrough

The Coffin card following the Mice card means the end of worries or finding a way out. The Sun following after the Coffin shows success at last:

Mice + Coffin + Sun

Client Example:

Question: Jason asked me, "How will my meeting with my ex-wife go?"

Mice + House + Cross =

Answer: Mice + House shows a stressful family situation, and the House + Cross combination shows a very heavy atmosphere

Question: Christine asked me: "What advice can you give me so that my project will be a success?"

Mice + Book + Whip + Sun + Key =

Answer: This is an advice reading, and the Mice says to pay attention to detail here. The Book stands for the project, and the Whip indicates that you should edit and go over it again/rewrite. The Sun + Key, in the end, shows it will be a great success.

Personal Example:

Before I moved back to New York City, I wanted to see how my move overall was going to be, and I pulled:

Mice + Stork + Ship = It turned out it was a very stressful move

Chapter Twenty-Eight

Card #24 - Heart - Jack of Hearts

No beauty shines brighter than that of a good heart.

The Heart card #24 is a **positive** card, but if negative cards follow after the Heart, the situation will turn into a negative one. The Heart card is one of the relationship cards. There are **3 relationship cards**: **Heart + Ring + Anchor**. It is always best to have all 3 relationship cards very close or close to the Man/Woman card. When I'm doing a Grand Tableau, and it's a relationship reading, I look for the placement of these cards and how far they are from the Significator card. This will show me how the relationship is going. I will explain that further in the Ring chapter.

- The core meaning of the Heart is **well-being**
- The Heart card symbolizes happy and joyful emotions
- It brings happiness to a reading
- Love, romance, and affection
- Understanding
- Compassion
- The heart card shows you what kind of feelings someone has for you (good or bad, depending on the surrounding cards)
- The Heart talks about true desires
- This card shows what our heart is beating for
- The Heart signifies contentment and satisfaction
- The Heart card is not a sign of commitment. To tell if it's a committed relationship, you need to examine the Grand Tableau in depth. I need to see cards like the Ring, Anchor, House, Tower, and Lilies next to the Heart that will show the commitment - the stability and longevity of this relationship.
- Always examine the surrounding cards of the Heart. It will show what kind of intention and faithfulness this person has.
- Having the Heart card as the very last card of a line reading indicates a delightful outcome.
- It can also describe your love for a family member, best friend, or heart's desires.

IN A RELATIONSHIP:

- A very loving and harmonious relationship

- Falling or being in love and caring for each other
- Lots of affection and romance
- Showing intense feelings for each other
- The one and only true love

DESCRIBING A PERSON:

- A very loving and caring person
- Compassionate
- A passionate and romantic person
- A person providing help for others
- Generous
- Optimistic, happy person
- A warm person with a big open heart
- A lovely-looking face with round cheekbones
- Curvy body type

HEALTH AND BODY PART:

- The heart organ
- The arteries
- Circularly system
- Cardiovascular disorders (the surrounding cards will describe the issue, especially if the Heart card is touching the Tree card in a health reading.)

MONEY:

- All is well with the finances

- A happy and stable financial situation
- It can refer to donations and charity

ADVICE:

- Be loving and compassionate
- Be happy
- Be generous
- Love yourself and others
- Follow your heart's desires

OBJECTS:

- Anything that looks like a heart
- Anything that has to do with love and romance

TIMING:

- Spring and Summer
- February (because of Valentine's Day)
- the 24th of the month

IN A GRAND TABLEAU, IF the Heart card is in the house of the Stork, that means there will be changes in love. Good or bad? Look where the Stork landed. For example, if the Stork landed in a negative house, that indicates there will be challenges in love.

IN A GRAND TABLEAU, IF the Coffin Card landed in the house of the Heart, that means there is no love.

IN A GRAND TABLEAU, IF THE HEARD CARD IS VERY CLOSE OR CLOSE TO THE SIGNIFICATOR CARD:

If the Significator is single, it could indicate a flirt. In order to say it is a stable and

committed relationship, we need the Ring for commitment and the Anchor for stability and loyalty very close to the Significator. Check which cards are touching the Heart; it will give you information about the love life of the Man/Woman card.

Now, if the Significator is married or in a relationship and the Heart card is close, that means love and passion between the couple is there. But if the Ring and Anchor are far away, that means there's no commitment and no stability in the relationship. In this case, it could be a relationship based on sex. **For a perfect relationship, we need all 3 relationship cards very close or close to the Significator.**

IN A GRAND TABLEAU, IF THE HEART CARD IS FAR OR VERY FAR FROM THE SIGNIFICATOR CARD:

For a single person, it indicates that there is no love for the duration of the spread. It can come with loneliness and an unfulfilled heart. It can also symbolize that there is not enough harmony, satisfaction, and joy in the Significator's life.

If the Significator is in a relationship and the Heart card is far or very far, this could mean that the love has diminished. The cards that surround the Heart will give you answers to what's going on. Negative cards around the Heart card indicate there are problems and complications in the relationship.

NOTE: Always set the intention before and while you are shuffling the cards what time frame this Grand Tableau is for!

Card Combination Examples:

- Heart + Sun = warm feelings, true love, a positive relationship

- Heart + Fish in a relationship reading, symbolizes a deep love with lots of emotions.

- Heart + Scythe = The End of a relationship (depending on the other card constellations). Most of the time, it stands for hurt feelings, painful feelings, or being hurt emotionally by somebody.

Client Examples:

Karina asked me: "Will I meet somebody new within the next 6 months?" I pulled:

Rider + Heart + Bouquet

Answer: Yes! The Rider indicates a new love is coming into one's life.

An interesting point was that Karina asked me this question in the month of November... When I saw the Bouquet card, I got the feeling that she would be meeting somebody new in the Spring, which matched the 6-month timeframe for this spread. Karina's feedback was positive - she met a new man in the Spring, and they started dating.

Wendy asked me: "Where will the relationship with my boyfriend go?" I pulled:

Crossroads + Heart + Coffin + Snake + Lilies

Answer: This relationship will end. I got the feeling because of another woman (Snake + Lilies). I hoped to see a positive card following the Coffin that would indicate a reconciliation (for example, Coffin + Clover), but having the Snake after the Coffin makes the situation more negative. Coffin + Snake = enemy, very negative influences.

Snake + Lilies = Disloyalty

Wendy called me 4 months later, saying they broke up because of another woman.

Daniel asked me: "Will my girlfriend move in with me, and if yes, when?"

NOTE: Always answer 1 question at a time!

So, I asked first if she would be moving in with Daniel, and I pulled:

Heart + Key + Tree =

Answer: Yes, she will be moving in, but it will take time.

It was beautiful how the cards showed me with the Tree card, without even asking, that it would take time. I got the feeling within 1 to 5 years (because the Tree is a timing card).

3 years later, my client Daniel contacted me to inform me that they finally moved in together! I was so happy to hear this; sometimes, predictions take a long time to evolve. **Be patient, and keep journaling your readings!**

Client Jennifer asked: "How will my get-together with my friend go?" I pulled:

Whip + Coffin + Bouquet + House + Heart

There will be an argument or disagreement, which will be ended by the Coffin. After the Coffin, we have the beautiful bouquet; that means happiness returns, and all is well!

Whip = argument, disagreement, discord

Coffin = ending or illness (depending on the context)

Bouquet = Happiness, surprise, gift

House = Family, home

Heart = Love, happiness, harmony

Having the heart card at the end of the line told me it would be a delightful outcome.

Chapter Twenty-Nine

Card #25 - Ring - Ace of Clubs

Without commitment you cannot have depth in anything.

- Neil Strauss -

The Ring card #25 is a **positive** card, BUT negative cards following the Ring make it negative.

- The core meaning of the Ring is **union**

- The Ring symbolizes a commitment, a marriage, a relationship, a partnership

- A bond

- A promise

- A cycle

- It can stand for a contract, a deal, or agreements

- Something reaches a completion

- It represents cycles, and something is recurring

- In a yes/no question, the Ring says YES!

- A repetitive situation (whether good or bad is described by the surrounding cards)

- Having the Ring as the last card in a line reading indicates a positive outcome

IN A RELATIONSHIP:

- **If the Ring is on the right side** of the Significator card, it indicates that the Man/Woman is sincere and ready to commit. Positive cards around the Ring show us that this relationship is a happy one. The couple has a strong bond (but check where the Heart and Anchor landed!)

- The cards around the Ring will give information on what's going on in this relationship. Negative cards around the Ring describe the problems and complications the relationship has.

- **If the Ring is on the left side** of the Significator card, it indicates that the Man/Woman is already attached to someone else.

- For a single person, the Ring to the right indicates a new relationship is coming into one's life, especially if the Rider or Dog was activated as a new person and is touching the Ring with other positive cards.

- The closer the Ring falls to the Significator card and to the right, the better it is; it indicates a strong connection. But if the Ring lands to the left and far away from the Man/Woman card, that shows us there is some work to do. It means the commitment is out of control for the duration of this spread. Don't forget what I mentioned earlier. **For a perfect relationship, we need all 3 relationship cards (Heart, Ring, Anchor) very close or close to the Significator card.**

- Having the Ring **on top or below** the Significator card means the relationship needs some attention. The Ring can easily shift to the right or to the left in the next Grand Tableau. The surrounding cards will give you information about what is going on.

DESCRIBING A PERSON:

- This is a very faithful person

- Reliable

- Dependable

- Responsible

- Committed

- Married, in a relationship

- Body type: curvy, round

NOTE: Never forget it is all about the context and the question!

For example:

If I ask what kind of personality this person has (I'm asking for a description of somebody's character) and I get the Ring, we can say he/she is a faithful, reliable, dependable, etc. person.

But if the question changes to: "Is this man serious about me?"

And we get Ring + Man + Heart + Book

Here, we see the Ring landed on the left side of the man, which means he is already attached to somebody else. He has feelings (Heart) for you but wants to keep it secret.

HEALTH AND BODY PART:

- Hands and fingers
- A chronic disease
- Reoccurring health matter
- A routine check-up
- Treatments that will be done over and over again
- It can be a health-related contract
- In a health reading, Ring + Moon = The menstrual cycle
- In a health reading, Bear + Ring = Gastric bypass

MONEY:

- Money comes in through a contract
- Money flows in through a business deal
- An agreement
- A joint account
- The financial situation is secure **(but it all depends on the surrounding cards - one card doesn't talk; the Lenormand tells you stories when the cards are connected and interact with each other!)**

ADVICE:

- Be loyal
- Commit
- Be dedicated

- Be responsible

- Reconnect

- If somebody asks: "Shall I sign this contract?" And you get the Ring...The answer is YES, go for it!

OBJECTS:

- A ring

- Jewelry

- Anything that has value and is binding

- Any object that is round and looks like a ring

- It can also be a place where you keep your jewelry

TIMING:

- The 25th of the month

- In my readings, I have noticed that when I ask for timing, and the Ring shows up, it has to do with my client's important dates. In other words, it will happen on a significant date, for example, an anniversary (any date that is important to the client - so you have to ask your client!)

IN A GRAND TABLEAU, IF the Whip card lands in the house of the Ring, that means there are difficulties in the relationship.

IN A GRAND TABLEAU, IF THE RING IS VERY CLOSE OR CLOSE TO THE SIGNIFICATOR CARD:

When I do a Grand Tableau for a relationship, I first look where the Ring landed. Close or far from the Man/Woman card, and it is very important to note on which side the Ring landed to the right or to the left of the Man/Woman card. Next, I examine the cards around the Ring. This will tell you a story of what the circumstances in the relationship are. If the Ring is over or under the Significator, that means the Man/Woman is thinking about the relationship or dealing with a relationship issue. Again, the cards around the

Ring will tell you what is going on.

IN A GRAND TABLEAU, IF THE RING IS FAR OR VERY FAR FROM THE SIGNIFICATOR:

Having the Ring in these positions indicates that right now, there is no stable, committed relationship for the duration of this spread. The further away the card is, the less control the Significator has. Also, it is very important to look where the other 2 relationship cards are (Heart and Anchor). The Significator might have a relationship, but they just live together like roommates. In this case, the Heart card is usually far away because there are no feelings involved. You always need to look at the whole picture. The cards around the Heart, Ring, and Anchor will describe what kind of relationship it is. For a couple, if the Ring lands on the left side and is far or very far away, that predicts difficulties in this relationship.

Client Examples:

Sandy asked: "Shall I go on further dates with this new man?" I pulled:

Ring + Crossroads + Coffin =

Answer: No, it will lead to a dead end.

Ken asked: "Where will my relationship lead in the future?" I pulled:

Tree + Anchor + Clouds + Sun + Moon =

Answer: You guys will be staying together in a long-term relationship (Tree + Anchor), but there will be many doubts and uncertainties that will clear (Clouds + Sun = remember that the Sun is the only card that can neutralize the Clouds). There will be harmony and success, and all will be well.

Question: "What are his intentions?"

Man + Ring + Anchor =

Answer: He wants to commit to and have a long-term relationship with you.

Chapter Thirty

Card #26 - Book - 10 of Diamonds

Listen to silence.

It has so much to say.

- Rumi -

The Book card #26 is a **neutral** card. The surrounding cards influence it.

• The core meaning of the Book is **the unknown**

- The Book card symbolizes secrets, knowledge, projects
- It tells us about things we don't know yet
- The cards around the Book will reveal the secret
- It stands for school, education, studies and learning
- Sometimes, the Book comes up for me as messages and information
- It can also represent a literal book, a magazine, or even a deck of cards
- Publishing and writing
- Training and courses

IN A RELATIONSHIP:

- A secret relationship
- You are learning about your relationship
- Things about your partner are not all revealed
- Hidden feelings for somebody
- A secret admirer
- Somebody has a secret
- A secret affair

DESCRIBING A PERSON:

- An intelligent person
- A student
- Likes to learn and read
- A shy and reserved person

- An introvert

- People who feel more comfortable focusing on their inner thoughts

- A person who is hiding his/her feelings

- Secretive

HEALTH AND BODY PART:

- The Brain

- Memory

- The eyes

- The health issue is not known yet

- Research, examinations, test results

- Health study

- Medical files

- **In a health reading,** Book + Mice = Memory loss

- **In a health reading,** Book + Scythe = Brain damage or brain surgery

MONEY:

- Your Bank account

- Look for hidden charges and fees

- Hidden money

ADVICE:

- Silence is true wisdom

- Go within

- Keep it for yourself
- Don't say anything
- Study and learn new things
- Research
- There is more to discover in this situation...

OBJECTS:

- A book
- Newspapers, magazines, notebooks
- A deck of cards
- It could also be a small box that looks like a book. Remember, the language of the Lenormand is symbolic!
- Book stores
- Library
- Schools
- Anything that has to do with learning

TIMING:

- The timing is not ready to be revealed
- Unknown...ask another time
- The 26th of the month

IN A GRAND TABLEAU, IF the Book card is in the house of the Scythe, that can mean the Significator is starting a new chapter in one's life. Next, you would look at what card landed in the house of the Book. For example, if it's the Heart card, then the new chapter has to do with love.

IN A GRAND TABLEAU, IF THE BOOK IS VERY CLOSE OR CLOSE TO THE SIGNIFICATOR CARD:

The Book indicates some unknown information. The closer the Book is to the Significator, the bigger the secret. Check the cards that surround the Book as they will give you information about the unknown - especially the card that lies directly under the Book reveals the secret, and the card above the book explains the secret. Sometimes, we just don't know the whole story about a situation. Also, check if there are any people cards around the book that have something to do with the secret.

But what the Book represents for an individual depends on the context and the question. For example, if I'm doing a reading for a student, I look around the Book to see what is going on in the area of education. Or, another example, if my client is working on a specific project, I look around the Book for information about this project.

Another very interesting thing I look for is which side of the Book faces the Significator - the spine or the open side. If the spine faces the Man/Woman card, it means the secret will remain hidden. But if the open side faces the Man/Woman, this means the secret will be discovered. For good or bad, it depends on the surrounding cards.

I also check which card follows after the Book. For example, Book + Sun or Book + Scythe means the secret will be revealed. On the other hand, if we get Book + Coffin or Book + Anchor, it means the secret is buried/the secret doesn't come out.

IN A GRAND TABLEAU, IF THE BOOK IS FAR OR VERY FAR FROM THE SIGNIFICATOR CARD:

In these positions, the unknown information is not as important. Check which cards are around the Book to get more information. Also, before I start a Grand Tableau, I ask my client if there are any specific topics my client wants to know about so I can charge/activate the cards to represent a particular subject. For example, I activate the Book card in my mind to represent a work project or education, etc.

Client Example:

Some time ago, I did a Grand Tableau for my client, Betty...She wanted to learn more about this new guy she started dating. She had a feeling that he was hiding something from her. So, with this context, I activated the Book card to represent the secret this guy is holding. Once the Grand Tableau was on the table, I looked to see which card lay directly under the Book, and it was the Ring. So that gave us immediately the answer to the secret: This guy is hiding a relationship he's in. The card above the Book is the Coffin, which indicates that the relationship he was in ended. A couple of months later Betty confirmed that the guy she is dating is still married, but he is in the process of ending this relationship. He was afraid to tell Betty the truth in the beginning that he was still married; he was afraid of losing her because of his circumstances.

Personal Examples:

Whenever my boyfriend surprised me with a visit, I would get in my daily draw:

Rider + Book + Bouquet + Heart + Lilies

I read this line like this:

Rider + Book = A surprise visit

Book + Bouquet = A beautiful surprise

Bouquet + Heart + Lilies = Is an auspicious love combination

I got this combination an endless number of times, and I knew he was coming that day!

Sometimes, in a line reading, if I get the Book as the very last card, that means the answer is still hidden. In other words, the cards tell me: Ask another time!

The day I started to write this book, I drew cards in the morning to see what I could expect that day. A couple of cards just flew out of the deck while I was shuffling:

Ship + Stars + Book + Moon + Sun

When I saw this line, I had no clue what it meant. I didn't think of writing a book. In the evening, after my meditation, I got this sudden impulse to start writing a Lenormand book, and at that moment, I started writing! Interesting how the cards showed this:

Ship + Stars = a new direction for me

The Book card landed in the middle as the focus card sandwiched between the Stars and the Moon, indicating divination for me. Having the Sun card at the end of the line shows me that this Book will be a success! Also, having all 3 luminaries (Stars, Moon, and Sun) is very auspicious for one's success and recognition, and it affirms that plans and projects are going in the right direction.

Chapter Thirty-One

Card #27 - Letter - 7 of Spades

*Let us never
underestimate the power
of a well-written letter.*

- Jane Austen -

The letter card #27 is a **neutral** card. It is highly influenced by the surrounding cards for good or for bad.

- The core meaning of the letter is **communication**

- The letter symbolizes all forms of written communication: letters, emails, faxes, text messages, and messages on any social media platform, for example, Facebook Messenger, WhatsApp, etc.

- It stands for any form of paperwork like tickets, bills, receipts, written notes, documents, certificates, reports, etc.

- The cards that surround the letter influence it, either good or bad. The cards that are touching the letter will give you information about what the letter is about.

IN A RELATIONSHIP:

- In a relationship context, if the letter is surrounded by positive cards like the Heart or the Moon card, it talks about love letters, passionate notes, or text messages

- It can stand for a long-distance relationship, for example, Ship + Letter + Heart

- Romantic and affectionate messages

- It can be a Valentine's Day card

- Surrounded by negative cards, it could be an end of communication, for example, Letter + Scythe or Letter + Coffin

DESCRIBING A PERSON:

- This person communicates well

- Somebody who shows a clear and forceful expression

- A speaker

- A writer

- Somebody who loves to write - a wordsmith, one who wrestles with words and wins!

- Very social

- A thin, slim person

HEALTH AND BODY PART:

- Any type of medical correspondence

- Test results

- X-rays

- Prescription

- Doctor referrals

- Fine motor skills related to hands and fingers

- People with a learning disorder (for example, dyslexia - having difficulties learning to read)

- In a health context, Ring + Letter can stand for a medical agreement

- A medical bill: Tree + Letter + Fish = Tree stands for health and the Fish for finances

MONEY:

- A check

- Depending on the cards around the letter, it could be a bill that's coming in the mail, or it could be a bank statement

- An envelope filled with money

ADVICE:

- Use your words wisely!

- Communicate in any form!

OBJECTS:

- Letters
- A card
- Newspapers
- A check
- Anything in paper form
- The letter, together with the Tower card, can stand for a post office

TIMING:

- The 27th of the month

IN A GRAND TABLEAU, IF THE LETTER CARD IS VERY CLOSE OR CLOSE TO THE SIGNIFICATOR CARD:

If the Letter card falls very close or close to the Significator card, an important message is coming. Check if the letter is in front of the Man/Woman card. This indicates the message is coming soon (in the future), or if the letter is behind the Man/Woman card in the past, that means the message was received already. Now, the cards surrounding the Letter card will describe the nature of the message. Positive cards around the letter indicate pleasant news, but negative cards around the letter guarantee bad news.

According to the traditional instructions of the Lenormand, the Clouds card will tell you if it's good or bad news. Look which side of the Clouds is turned towards the Significator card. If the dark side of the Clouds faces the Man/Woman card, it will be bad news, but if the light side of the Clouds faces the Man/Woman card, it will be good news.

Now, if the dark side of the Clouds is facing the Significator but positive cards surround the Letter, you should instead focus on the cards that surround the letter because the Clouds rule is neutralized. Now, if the dark side of the Clouds is facing the Significator and the Letter is surrounded by negative cards, that means bad news is on its way guaranteed. I personally focus only on the cards that surround the letter. They will give me insight into the kind of message (good or bad).

If the Letter is close, the message will come from your close surroundings. Check which

Life Area cards and people cards are around the letter. This will give you information on where the message is coming from and what the message is about.

IN A GRAND TABLEAU, IF THE LETTER CARD IS FAR OR VERY FAR FROM THE SIGNIFICATOR CARD:

This means the message is coming from afar (not your immediate surroundings), or it is not very important for this particular reading.

Card Combination Examples:

The Letter card in combination with:

- Tower = Formal, official news
- Sun = Positive, happy news
- Clover = Lottery ticket
- Ship = Flight ticket
- House = Message from family
- Snake = Very negative information that brings complications
- Stars = Comes up in my reading as lots of messages like texting back and forth

Client Examples:

My client Diana asked me: "What kind of message will I receive about my health checkup? I pulled:

Tree + Letter + Cross =

Answer: Unfortunately, it will be bad news. The Tree affirms the health context, and the letter is health-related news, which is very negative (Cross).

Jake was waiting for a specific letter regarding his finances. So, I activated the Letter card while I was shuffling. After I was done shuffling, I flipped the deck over and looked for the Letter card in the deck, and then I pulled the cards that sandwiched the letter in (I pulled one card that came before the Letter and one card that came after the Letter):

Bear + Letter + Mice =

The Bear here stands for the finances, and the Mice represent stress and worries. So, my answer to Jake was: The news about your finances will be very stressful and worrisome.

Susan asked me: "Will I get the promotion at my job?"

Clouds + Sun + Fox + Letter + Key =

Answer: The Clouds card, in the beginning, shows the confusion and the doubts about the promotion, but the Sun will clear all the doubts. The Fox card in the middle of the line is our focus card and represents work. The Letter followed by the Key is a definite YES answer. Susan got the promotion!

Chapter Thirty-Two

Card #28 and #29 - Man - Ace of Hearts & Woman - Ace of Spades

The Man card #28 represents either the male Significator who is asking for the reading **OR** it represents a specific man for a female client who is getting the reading. It can be a boyfriend, husband, partner, lover, etc. Before you start the reading, ask your client who the important people in their lives are so you can charge/activate the people cards to represent a specific person. In other words, give the Man/Woman cards a name, for example, Mary (the client) and John (Mary's husband).

The Woman card #29 represents either the female Significator who is asking for the reading **OR** a specific woman for the male client who is getting the reading. It can be a girlfriend, wife, partner, lover, etc. **Once again, don't forget** to charge the Significator cards to represent a specific person before you start shuffling!

Both Man and Woman cards are neutral and are highly influenced by the surrounding cards.

The Man card also talks about the masculine energy and the left brain. The Woman card represents the feminine energy and the right brain. The cards around the Man/Woman card describe their character.

The cards in front of the Man/Woman card on the right side show the future, and the cards behind the Man/Woman on the left side show the past. The cards above and below the Man/Woman show the present.

IN A GRAND TABLEAU:

If the Man/Woman card lands all the way on the bottom of the Grand Tableau, it could mean that the Significator is under a lot of pressure. Life is weighing the Significator down. All the cards are pressing heavily down on the Significator. Look to see which card is above the head. This will show you what the Man/Woman is thinking about. Most of the time, there are negative cards close by. Check which Life Area cards (work, relationships, health...) are close to the Significator. This will give you clues as to what the problems might be. It could also indicate that the Significator does not have much control over his/her life at the moment.

If the Man/Woman cards lands at the top of the Grand Tableau, that means the Significator has control over his/her life. Even if there are negative card constellations around, it's always best to be on top!

If the Significator card lands in the first column of the Grand Tableau (the first vertical row), that means there was a life-changing event, and the Significator started a brand-new chapter in his/her life. The cards around the Significator will give hints, especially if the Stork card is also in the first column. Check which cards are surrounding the Stork, as they will tell you what kind of changes occurred.

Another possibility is that the Significator is too focused on the future and wants to leave the past behind. In that case, **if the Significator landed in the first column** of the Grand Tableau, it is not possible to see what happened in the past because there are no cards behind the Man/Woman card. Here, I would use an old **counting technique**. I start counting from the Significator card backward on **a count of 7**. The seventh card I land on will be marked as the first card of the Significator's past. Then I start counting again, starting from the card I just landed on. I continue this until I end up on the Significator card. So, in the end, I have 5 cards that will give me information about my client's **past**.

THE LENORMAND

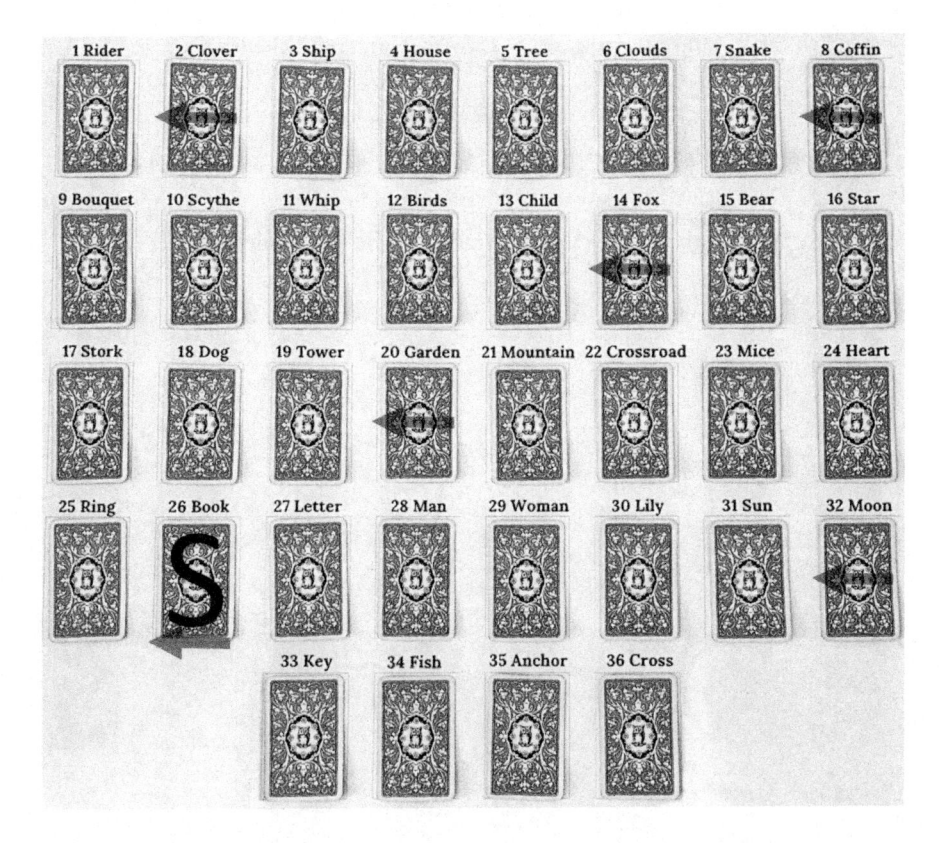

1 Rider	2 Clover	3 Ship	4 House	5 Tree	6 Clouds	7 Snake	8 Coffin
9 Bouquet	10 Scythe	11 Whip	12 Birds	13 Child	14 Fox	15 Bear	16 Star
17 Stork	18 Dog	19 Tower	20 Garden	21 Mountain	22 Crossroad	23 Mice	24 Heart
25 Ring	26 Book	27 Letter	28 Man	29 Woman	30 Lily	31 Sun	32 Moon
		33 Key	34 Fish	35 Anchor	36 Cross		

IN A GRAND TABLEAU, IF THE SIGNIFICATOR CARD LANDED IN THE 8TH COLUMN (THE LAST VERTICAL ROW):

Having the Man/Woman card in this position may indicate that the Significator is living in the past, and there are still issues that are not resolved - this is why the cards are not showing a future just yet. The Significator has to make certain decisions and take action; then, the future will be written. Also, it means that the Man/Woman is ending a life chapter and is going to start a new one.

Always check if the Stork and the Crossroads are also in the 8th column. This means there is a significant change for the Man/Woman coming up. The cards around the Stork, Crossroads, and Significator will give information about the change that's about to occur. In this case, I use the counting technique again, but this time, I count **starting from the Significator card on a count of 7 forward.**

Every 7th card I land on will give me information about the future.

Once again, the 7th card you land on is the starting point for the next counting, and so on, until you land where you started (The Significator card). By the way, you can use the counting technique with any other card to get more information. For example, you can start counting from the House card to get more insight into family matters.

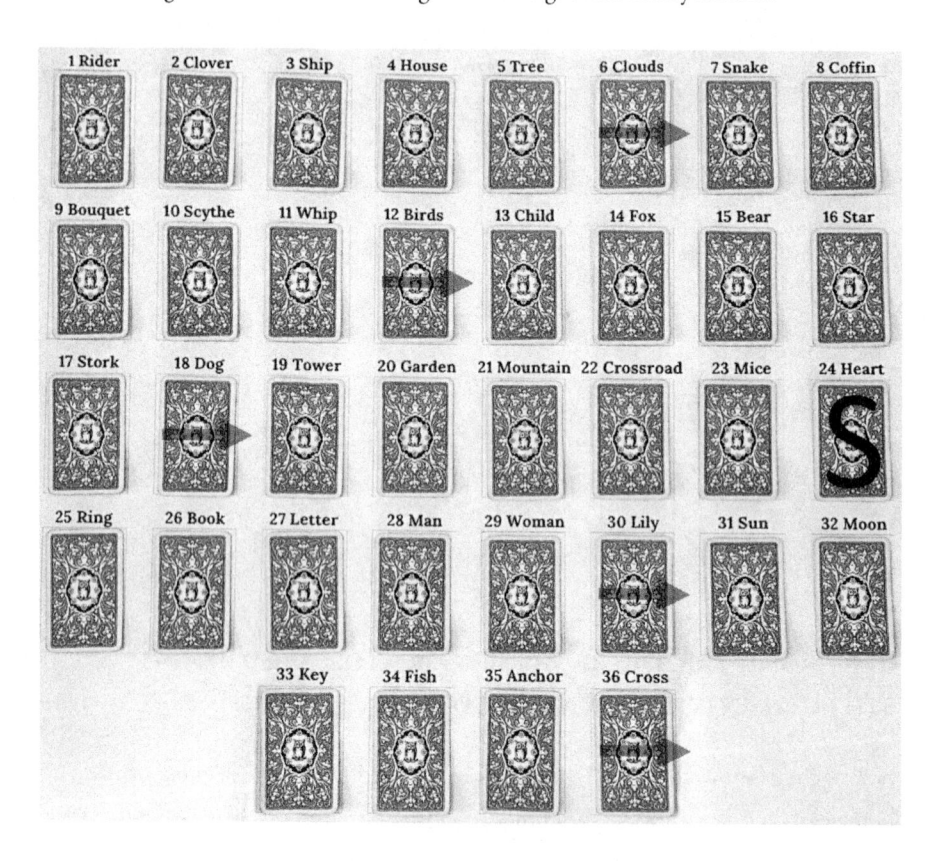

1 Rider	2 Clover	3 Ship	4 House	5 Tree	6 Clouds	7 Snake	8 Coffin
9 Bouquet	10 Scythe	11 Whip	12 Birds	13 Child	14 Fox	15 Bear	16 Star
17 Stork	18 Dog	19 Tower	20 Garden	21 Mountain	22 Crossroad	23 Mice	24 Heart S
25 Ring	26 Book	27 Letter	28 Man	29 Woman	30 Lily	31 Sun	32 Moon
		33 Key	34 Fish	35 Anchor	36 Cross		

Some readers would reshuffle the cards if the Man/Woman card landed in the 8th column because they want more cards in front of the Significator to be able to predict the future. I never reshuffle the cards because they landed like this for a reason. I am not going against the will of the cards!

One time in the past, I reshuffled, and the Significator landed in the same spot 3 times!!! Since then, I understood what the cards were trying to tell me:

Never reshuffle the cards; there is a reason why they landed like this! So, when that happens, use the counting technique to get insights about the future or the past!

IF THE SIGNIFICATOR CARD LANDS IN THE MIDDLE OF THE GRAND TABLEAU:

That means the Man/Woman has a lot going on in their life. The cards that touch the Significator will give information about what is happening in one's life. If the Significator lands in the middle but on top of the Grand Tableau, this means he/she is in control of what's going on. But if the Significator lands in the middle and on the bottom of the Grand Tableau, this means he/she has no control over what's going on.

Man/Woman Card in Combination With:

- Significator card + Ship = the Man/Woman might be a foreigner or a change is coming
- Tree = The Significator may be dealing with health problems
- Bouquet = An attractive person
- Birds = The Significator communicates well
- Stork = A Man/Woman who is graceful and has an uplifting personality
- Tower = The Significator may be lonely and isolated
- Garden = The Significator may be single, a social butterfly
- Mountain = A stubborn, lonely person
- Mice = The person is stressed and anxious
- Significator + Ring = This person is ready to commit
- Ring + Significator = This person is already in a commitment
- Sun = A happy person

- Anchor = This person is reliable

- Cross = A burdened and exhausted person

Chapter Thirty-Three

Card #30 - Lilies - King of Spades

*Patience is not simply
the ability to wait -
it's how we behave
while we're waiting.*

- Joyce Meyer -

The Lilies card #30 is a **neutral** card. If it's looked at alone, it is positive, but depending on the cards that touch the Lilies card, it can be positive or negative.

- The core meaning of the Lilies is **satisfaction**

- The circumstances you are in need A LOT OF PATIENCE

- This is a timing card

- It symbolizes wisdom, knowledge, and respect

- Things need time to mature and to grow

- The Lilies card is a state of being calm, peaceful, and untroubled

- Depending on the context and the question, the Lilies card can also stand for family (aunts and uncles - or elderly) and peace and harmony at home

- The Lilies can stand for a wise person with a lot of experience

- The Lilies talks about somebody's virtue; it's showing somebody's behavior and moral standards

- When I am answering questions about matters of the heart, the Lilies card always shows up in my readings (for good or bad, depending on the placement and the surrounding cards)

- A couple of years ago, I did a card reading for a client who was going through a court case. The Lilies are a symbol of the French monarchy (fleur-de-lis) and a symbol of high honor. Having the Lilies card at the end of a line reading together with positive cards shows that things are going to be fair and will be resolved peacefully, but it may take time and patience. They bring serenity to any situation.

IN A RELATIONSHIP:

- You will experience satisfaction in this relationship

- Joy and happiness

- An old romance

- You will meet somebody later in your life

THE LENORMAND

- You will grow old with this person

- You will meet a person that is older than you

- A mature and honest relationship

- You may have to be very patient with your partner before you can move forward together

NOTE: It all depends on the context, the question, and the specific situation the client is in!

DESCRIBING A PERSON:

- Attractive

- Sexy

- European looking

- Mature face

- May have grey hair

- Can be a mentor, a teacher

- An elderly established person

- The personality of this person is calm, peaceful, and serene

- This is an experienced person with a lot of knowledge and wisdom

HEALTH AND BODY PART:

- Age-related illnesses

- Aging

- Sexually transmitted diseases

- Alzheimer's

- Recovery and treatment may take a long time
- You need to rest

MONEY:

- Retirement
- Stocks and shares
- Investments
- Any money that's growing over time
- Be patient

ADVICE:

- Be patient
- Take your time
- Be calm
- Rest

OBJECTS:

- A Lily flower
- Anything that has to do with retirement
- Any place that has to do with relaxation (a spa)
- I got the Lilies card in my readings for subjects like death (Coffin + Lilies)

TIMING:

- Something will take a very long time
- Winter

- The 30th of the month

NOTE: The Lilies, the Bouquet, and the Child cards belong to the PROVIDENCE GROUP. These three cards will give you insight into your fate or what a higher power has in store for you.

IN A GRAND TABLEAU, IF the Lilies card landed in the house of the Mountain, that means there is no sexuality at the moment, or there are obstacles with one's sexuality.

IN A GRAND TABLEAU, IF THE LILIES CARD IS RIGHT ABOVE THE SIGNIFICATOR'S HEAD:

This is a sign of virtue. This means the Significator is a person who is honest and sincere, and one's behavior shows high moral standards. The Man/Woman will be rewarded by a higher power for being a good person and for having good intentions (karma). But be careful if you talk to your client about this subject - NOT everybody understands it or is ready to hear it. Your client might take it in a negative way. I only mention it if my client asks for it. **Lilies above the significator card is very positive - It shows one's virtue.**

1 Rider	2 Clover	3 Ship	4 House	5 Tree	6 Clouds	7 Snake	8 Coffin
9 Bouquet	10 Scythe	11 Whip	12 Birds	13 Child	14 Fox	15 Bear	16 Star
17 Stork	18 Dog	19 Tower	20 Garden	21 Mountain	22 Crossroad	23 Mice	24 Heart
25 Ring	26 Book	27 Letter	28 Man	29 Woman	30 Lily	31 Sun	32 Moon
		33 Key	34 Fish	35 Anchor	36 Cross		

The best constellation is having the Lilies together with the Bouquet above the Significator. It shows happiness and joy will come to one's life, and the Significator will be rewarded for his/her good intentions and appreciated for one's goodness.

THE LENORMAND

1 Rider	2 Clover	3 Ship	4 House	5 Tree	6 Clouds	7 Snake	8 Coffin
9 Bouquet	10 Scythe	11 Whip	12 Birds	13 Child	14 Fox	15 Bear	16 Star
17 Stork	18 Dog	19 Tower	20 Garden	21 Mountain	22 Crossroad	23 Mice	24 Heart
25 Ring	26 Book	27 Letter	28 Man	29 Woman	30 Lily	31 Sun	32 Moon
		33 Key	34 Fish	35 Anchor	36 Cross		

If the Lilies card lands directly under the Significator, the Man/Woman is stepping on the Lilies. This indicates that the Significator is doing something morally wrong. Dishonesty, infidelity, indecent behavior, or any wrongdoing are some examples. The surrounding cards will give you insight into what's going on. **Lilies below the significator card is negative - it shows the significator is doing something morally wrong.**

The Lilies below the Significator card is negative - it shows the Significator is doing something morally wrong.

The card right above the Lilies will tell you in which Life Area the Significator is acting improperly. The card below the Lilies is blessed.

If the Clouds card is next to the Lilies under the Significator, that means there will be some very unpleasant dramatic problems with people and situations in the client's life, which can lead to a separation.

Having the Lilies and the Clouds together above the Significator means there will be a lot of sadness in the domestic environment and family arguments. Especially if the dark side of the Clouds is facing the Lilies.

Another very bad constellation is Lilies and Scythe, which also indicates that one's peace at home will be very disturbed, and the people in one's environment can cause disputes.

Now, if the Lilies card lands somewhere far away from the Significator but still below, that means the Man/Woman is doing something wrong, but it's not as bad as having the Lilies directly below the Man/Woman. Having the Lilies somewhere far and below diminishes the negative impact.

But having the Child card near the Lilies neutralizes the negative effect. It means the Significator didn't do something intentionally wrong. It shows the Significator did something wrong because of immaturity, inexperience, or just being naive.

NOTE: When it comes to cheating, I see in readings very often the Fox card next to the Lilies, but to get more information, also check the houses...which card landed in the house of the Lilies and which card landed in the house of the Fox.

Client Examples:

Kerry asked me: "Will I be able to sell my house within the next 3 months?"

Tree + House + Lilies =

Answer: No, it will take time to sell the house. The House card is sandwiched in between the Tree and the Lilies; both are timing cards and indicate it will take a long time.

It took Kerry 1 year and 3 months to sell the house.

Nancy asked: "Will I be able to get the money back?"

Lilies + Cross + Key =

Answer: Yes, you will get your money back, but it will take a long time.

Lilies + Cross = Means the waiting is a burden; it indicates impatience.

Cross + Key = In the end, there will be success, and the Key is a definite yes answer.

Maria wanted to know why she got turned down from the management position she had applied many times:

Fox + Lilies + Mice + Rider

Answer: The Fox card stands for the job/position Maria applied for. The Lilies and the Mice indicate that there is a lack of experience; therefore, she doesn't qualify for this position.

Kevin asked me: "How should I handle the situation with my in-laws?"

Sun + Lilies =

Answer: Be confident (Sun), but stay calm and peaceful and give it some time (Lilies).

Ruth asked: "How will my meeting with my family go?"

Garden + House + Lilies =

Answer: Your meeting will be very peaceful and satisfying (Lilies).

The Garden stands for the gathering with the family (House).

When I do love readings the Lilies card always shows up. Here is an example of a perfect love combination: Lilies + Sun

On the other hand, Lilies + Coffin or Lilies + Mice can indicate one has problems with the relationship.

This was a draw for client Martha. On that day, Martha received an unexpected significant gift of money!

Lilies + Child + Crossroads + Garden + Letter + Fish + Bouquet

The Lilies, the Child, and the Bouquet cards are cards from the Providence group. The Crossroads and the Garden are two tree cards.

This combination of Providence cards + Tree cards followed by Letter + Fish + Bouquet is a very auspicious combination for money!

Chapter Thirty-Four

Card #31 - Sun - Ace of Diamonds

No matter

How tall

The mountain is,

It cannot block the sun.

- Chinese Proverb -

The Sun card #31 is a **positive** card. But it weakens if negative cards are following.

- The core meaning of the Sun is **life force, success, and joy**

- The Sun card symbolizes optimism, happiness, and a victory

- It brings light to negative readings; it brings clarity and confidence to overcome any obstacle

- The Sun card is the only card that can neutralize the Clouds; it eases the unfavorable impacts of the negative cards

- The Sun gives warmth and light to any situation

- The Sun, depending on the context and question, can talk about a new beginning

- In a yes/no question, the Sun says YES!

- Having the Sun in a line reading as the last card predicts the end of troubles and a very favorable outcome

- Goals will be reached, and success is guaranteed

- The Sun is a masculine card

IN A RELATIONSHIP:

- A warm relationship

- A blissful time together

- A positive, happy relationship

- A passionate relationship

DESCRIBING A PERSON:

- Blonde hair and light skin tone

- A positive person

- Optimistic

- An uplifting personality

- Happy

- A warm, friendly person

- An energetic person

- A famous person

- Attractive physical appearance

- Can be selfish, arrogant, self-centered and narcissistic

HEALTH AND BODY PART:

In a health context, if you are asking how the illness is going to develop, the Sun talks about recovery and healing. It symbolizes vibrant health and vitality. But if you are asking about a specific diagnosis, the Sun can represent the following:

- Overheating and dehydration

- Sunburn, heat stroke

- Vitamin D levels

- The Sun also stands for all kinds of scans (x-rays, MRI)

- The Sun stands for one's energy levels; with negative cards, the energy level is decreasing

- In a health context, when the Tree card is around and with negative cards following the Sun, it can talk about some deficiencies, for example, Vitamin D deficiency, for example, Tree + Sun + Mice

MONEY:

- Success

- Financial profits

- Winnings

- Money is coming in

- Positive outcomes

- Positive transactions that lead to a victory

ADVICE:

- Stay positive

- Be optimistic

- Go out in the sun

- Be confident and take charge of the situation

OBJECTS:

- The Sun

- A sunny place

- Anything that has to do with light and heat

TIMING:

- Summer

- Daytime

- The 31st of the month

IN A GRAND TABLEAU, IF THE SUN CARD IS VERY CLOSE OR CLOSE TO THE SIGNIFICATOR CARD:

Having the Sun close by the Significator is a very positive sign. It brings success and victory. The Sun enhances the effects of the other positive cards that are touching the Sun. Especially cards like the Lilies, Bouquet, Clover, Tree, and Garden will become more positive. The Man/Woman card has courage, and luck will be on one's side. Troubles will disappear. The surrounding cards will give information on what areas of life the favorable effects of the Sun will take place.

Also, it is best to have the Sun card above the Significator card rather than below. That way, it will shine down on the Man/Woman card with its positivity.

IN A GRAND TABLEAU, IF THE SUN CARD IS FAR OR VERY FAR FROM THE SIGNIFICATOR:

In these positions, the Sun rays cannot reach the Significator, and the positive effects of the Sun are out of reach. But check which cards the Sun is touching and influencing. The Man/Woman might be discouraged, and success is unreachable for the duration of the spread.

If negative cards follow the Sun, it means the positive effects of the Sun are blocked, and your luck is fading away.

If positive cards follow the Sun, it means there will be an end to all troubles and pain. It announces success no matter how bad the situation is.

Card Combination Examples:

- Sun + Whip = Competition
- Sun + Child = A new beginning
- Sun + Bouquet = Happiness and Joy
- Coffin + Sun = Reconciliation
- Sun + Coffin = The outcome will be unfavorable
- COFFIN + SUN in a relationship reading: This combination always plays out as a reconciliation or a happy ending.

Client Example:

Question: Kelly asked me: "Will I receive the salary raise?"

Sun + Fish + Mice =

Answer: Yes, you will receive a raise, but not what you expected; it will be less.

Personal Example:

Here is an example of a daily draw:

The Lenormand can be very literal at times.

Sun 31 + Crossroads 22 + Tree 5 + Tower 19 + Letter 27

On that sunny day (31), I was on the road (22) to the pharmacy (5+19) to pick up my prescription (27). The commute was successful (31).

The focus card here is the TREE card #5, so it's health-related.

The TOWER card #19 next to the tree here represents a health building like a pharmacy. The letter in the end showed me I would receive my prescription. Having the SUN card #31 at the beginning with no negative cards in that line told me that my day was going to be a success, and it was!

Chapter Thirty-Five

Card #32 - Moon - 8 of Hearts

Like a beautiful moon,
We must go through phases
Of emptiness
To feel full again.

The Moon card #32 is a **positive** card, BUT it turns negative when around negative cards.

- The core meaning of the Moon is **honor, reputation, and recognition**

- The Moon is a very romantic card

- The Moon stands for fame and public recognition

- It represents the natural cycles, for example, the menstrual cycle and motherhood

- The Moon is a feminine card

- Having the Moon in a work-project question, it talks about success and being recognized and rewarded

- The Moon talks about our emotions, our dreams, and our intuition

- The Moon can also stand for psychic abilities and intuition

IN A RELATIONSHIP:

- This connection is full of love and romance

- Emotional passion

- Strengthening one's bond

- Flirtation

- A romantic date

- Attraction and harmony

- Deep affection

- Depending on the card combination, it can be an engagement (Moon + Ring)

- For a single person, it could mean a new romantic partner is coming into one's life

- A romantic evening, deep love (= Heart + Moon)

- To seek the affection or love of someone (wooing)

- In combination with positive cards, it talks about love, romance, affection, and blissful emotions

NOTE: The cards that touch the Moon will give more insight into the characteristics! One card doesn't talk alone; it's the combination of cards that form the sentences!

DESCRIBING A PERSON:

- Pale skin tone; porcelain skin
- Alluring, beautiful-looking
- Powerfully and mysteriously attractive
- Seductive
- Loving - touchy-feely, lovey-dovey
- Captivating
- Round face
- Could be a famous or well-known person
- Creative
- Poetic
- Inventive
- Can be an artist, a psychic, or a psychiatrist
- A spiritual person
- An emotional person
- Sentimental
- Can be moody

HEALTH AND BODY PART:

- The hormones
- The female organs
- Natural cycles like the menstrual cycle
- PMS
- Menopause
- The psyche, the emotional state of mind
- Can stand for a pregnancy if in combination with Stork, Child, Tree, Garden, and Anchor

MONEY:

- An unstable financial situation (an up and down like ebb and flow - But it really depends on the surrounding card combinations; if surrounded by very positive cards, it can also be talking about new doors opening to money-making opportunities)

ADVICE:

- Listen to your intuition
- Go within
- Meditate
- Dream, visualize, believe
- Expose yourself
- Make yourself visible to others
- Be creative

OBJECTS:

- The Moon

- Anything that looks like a Moon or has a moon shape

- A romantic place

- Anything that has to do with your bed

- A lamp

- Anything that has to do with fame, for example, a cinema

TIMING:

- In the evening, at night

- During the moon cycles

- With the ebb and flow of the tides

IN A GRAND TABLEAU, IF THE MOON CARD IS VERY CLOSE OR CLOSE TO THE SIGNIFICATOR:

If the Moon card lands close to the Significator card, that means there is recognition and sincere appreciation for the Man/Woman coming. Respect and applause from other people will be received.

Acknowledgments and great honors may be within reach. The surrounding cards will give insight into the subject. The Moon card is a positive card, but the cards touching it have a great influence on it. If a lot of negative cards are surrounding the Moon or if the Moon lands in a negative house of the Grand Tableau, that means there will be a lot of emotional and mental stresses, worries, anxiety, and pressure.

IN A GRAND TABLEAU, IF THE MOON CARD IS FAR OR VERY FAR FROM THE SIGNIFICATOR:

In these positions, the Moon card tells us there will be a lack of appreciation and respect for the Man/Woman card.

Unfortunately, the recognition is out of reach for the duration of this spread. It also indicates there will be sadness and grief for the Significator, a feeling of deep distress caused by loss, disappointment, or other misfortune. Important are the surrounding cards! They will tell you the story of what is going on. Hopefully, there are enough other positive cards surrounding the Man/Woman. Another important thing I look for in a Grand Tableau is if the Moon is surrounded by negative cards. I check if there are any negative people cards around the Moon - for example, the Fox, the Mice, or the Mountain... There might be negative people around who talk bad behind your back and may ruin your reputation.

Also, it is best to have the Moon card above the Significator card rather than below. The Moon, like the other luminaries (Stars and Sun), belongs in the sky. That way, they can shine down on the Man/Woman card with its positive effects.

IN A GRAND TABLEAU, IF the Significator lands in the house of the Moon, it indicates that the Man/Woman is a sensitive person.

Card Combination Examples:

In a relationship context:

- Moon + Scythe = An emotional break up, being emotionally hurt
- Moon + Heart = Love and romance
- Moon + Ring = Can be a proposal

In a health context:

- Moon + Scythe = An abortion (if the Child and Tree is close)
- Moon + Tree = Hormones, your mood and state of mind
- Moon + Stork = Can indicate a pregnancy if the Child and Anchor are close
- Clouds + Moon = Depression, moodiness

In a work context:

- Moon + Sun = Success, a recognition, fame
- Moon + Stars = Goals are being reached, success, recognition and awards, fame

Client Examples:

Kevin is very worried about a work project that is connected with a promotion and an increase in salary. He wanted to know what the end result would be for him. I did a line of 7:

Clouds + Mice + Tower + Sun + Moon + Anchor + Fish

The Clouds and the Mice card shows Kevin's confusion and anxiety; it is a stressful situation for him at the company he is working for, represented by the Tower. But then we have the Sun and the Moon, which predicts his success and recognition and is followed by a very stable financial situation. The Fish stands here for his finances, and the Anchor shows a stable, long-term financial situation.

Six weeks later, Kevin called me with the happy news that his project had been a success and that he had been promoted!

Kate asked me: "Will I have money coming in next month?"

Ring + Moon + Heart = That is a yes answer. Kate did receive an unexpected windfall from her ex-boyfriend.

Chapter Thirty-Six

Card #33 - Key - 8 of Diamonds

Don't give up. Normally it is the last key on the ring which opens the door.
- Paulo Coelho -

The Key card #33 is a **positive** card.

- The core meaning of the Key is **success** and **solutions**

- When you have the Key, you can unlock doors to your goals and wishes

- It predicts a positive outcome

- The Key brings answers, and it shows you what is important

- In a yes/no question, the Key says YES!

- Having the Key after a series of negative cards is always a good omen because it announces the end of a period of misfortune; an unexpected turn of events is going to take place in a positive way. Solutions will be found to solve any problem. The Key will show you the way out of a negative situation and give you complete control; you can handle any situation if you have the Key.

- The Key stands for certainty, security, and safety

- Look at what cards are surrounding the Key as they point out the solution to a problem

IN A RELATIONSHIP:

- A loving, committed relationship that is built on a foundation of trust, and trust comes from honesty

- An important, significant relationship

- This is the right partner

- Two people feel they are linked on a soul level in a significant way

- A happy relationship

- Having the Key to someone's heart (Key + Heart = Soul mate)

- If there are any misunderstandings, they will be cleared quickly because the Key is giving answers, solutions, and understanding

DESCRIBING A PERSON:

- A skinny but strong person with some curves

- Attractive
- Active
- Neat
- A very important person in your life
- A thinker, highly intelligent with an analytical mind

HEALTH AND BODY PART:

- A healing
- Recovery
- All is well; there is nothing to worry about
- Can represent the collarbone

MONEY:

- New doors are opening for extra income
- New money-making opportunities appear
- The financial situation is very good
- The financial situation is secure
- Prosperity coming in
- If the financial situation is bad at the moment, and we get the Key, that means the situation will improve all of a sudden

ADVICE:

- Yes, go for it!
- You have the power to create your reality and unlock doors
- Act and take this new opportunity

- **OBJECTS:**

  - A key

  - A lock

  - A key card

  - Anything that is associated with a key, for example, a keychain

  - It can also represent an electronic code to get access

TIMING:

It's happening NOW!

IN A GRAND TABLEAU, IF THE KEY CARD IS VERY CLOSE OR CLOSE TO THE SIGNIFICATOR:

The Key card is one of the best cards in the deck. It is always very favorable to have the Key in the comfort zone (very close and close). The Key brings success, solutions, and positive outcomes. The Man/Woman has the Key to open the doors to new possibilities. The Significator is in charge of his/her destiny.

According to the old tradition, my mother taught me that having the Key close was a very positive sign. It meant a high social status for a male, especially if the Moon, Ship, Fish, and Anchor cards were close by, too. It shows that the man has a high social status and great wealth and can take care of his family. Now, the opposite is the case if the Key, Moon, Ship, Fish, and Anchor cards are far or very far from the Man card. This indicates dissatisfaction and a loss of reputation or respect. Losses are to follow.

Now, for a female, having the Key very close or close by is a promising sign for a happy marriage if the Heart, Ring, and Anchor cards are also close by. Having the Bouquet card in the mix can indicate a proposal.

If the Key is close to the Man/Woman card but is surrounded by negative cards, that means solutions will be within reach for those troubles.

Always examine the cards around the key, as they will point out the answers. If the Key is surrounded by positive cards and lands in a positive house, that is a very favorable card constellation. It predicts success, positive outcomes, and doors opening for the Significator. The Man/Woman has the green light to act on one's wishes and desires.

IN A GRAND TABLEAU, IF THE KEY CARD IS FAR OR VERY FAR FROM THE SIGNIFICATOR:

To have the Key in those positions means that success and solutions are for the duration of this spread out of reach. The Significator's efforts may fail, and it can lead to disappointments; troubles and losses may follow. But check which cards (especially Life Area cards) are around the Key - that will give you insight what is being positively influenced by the Key.

Card Combination Examples:

Clouds + Key = Solutions are found, the confusion and troubles will clear

Coffin + Key = The end of a negative time

Scythe + Key = Unexpected, very sudden success

Whip + Key = Argument will be solved

Child + key = A successful new start

Stork + key = An important change can be a move

Mountain + Key = Successfully overcoming an obstacle

Cross + Key = There will be a success after the hard times

Client Examples:

This was a reading for Mark, who had a lot of trouble with his ex-wife about child custody.

His question was: "Will we come to an agreement?"

For this reading, I chose the Rana George Lenormand deck with her 4 extra cards.

One of those extra cards is the Incense burner card #38, which showed up in the reading in a beautiful way. I pulled:

Whip + Tower + Mountain + Incense burner (card #38) + Key

The first two cards affirm the court case (Whip + Tower), which leads to a big obstacle (Mountain), but then we have the Incense burner card # 38, which talks about clearing, so in this case, we can say the obstacles will be cleared away, and a solution (Key) will be found. After 3 months, my client Mark called me to confirm that my prediction had come true. In the end, they found a solution, and all was well. My client said the reading helped him keep a positive attitude and gave him peace of mind that all would be well. I love messages like this; it makes me happy to help people in difficult times.

My client, Jennifer, was dissatisfied with her relationship. She asked me: "What advice can you give me?"

While I was shuffling the cards, 2 cards flew out:

Lilies + Key = This combination means patience is key! Solutions will be found in time for a long-term solution.

Chapter Thirty-Seven

Card #34 - Fish - King of Diamonds

Abundance in life is a reflection
Of abundant thoughts.
All you have to do is ask, trust, and
Allow yourself to receive.

The Fish card #34 is a **positive** card when looked at alone. However, it is influenced by its surrounding cards and can turn negative. The Fish card can also be a **neutral** card if it represents a business.

- The core meaning of the Fish card is **prosperity**

- The Fish card symbolizes wealth, abundance, independence and freedom, and the ability to let go

- It stands for plenty of....or a lot of something

- The Fish card can also represent your drinking habits

- For me, the Fish also talks about free flow; if a negative card follows the Fish, it stops the flow

- The Fish represents your finances (Money, cash flow)

- It is a card that talks about femininity and fertility

- The Fish enhances the effects of the positive cards, and it increases the negativity of the negative cards

- Having the Fish card close by tells us the Significator will be very successful in all his/her undertakings. The Fish brings a positive change to the reading.

- Together with positive cards, the Fish predicts freedom, unity, happiness, and good luck

- The Fish card represents self-employment and entrepreneurship; it can be a small business

- The Fish is associated with trade, commerce, import and export, and everything that has to do with sales, purchases, and transactions

- If I'm doing a reading and the client is asking specifically about a certain business, I charge the Fish card to represent the business

- In a love context, the Fish can stand for one's emotions. For example, Heart + Fish = lots of emotions, a deep love

IN A RELATIONSHIP:

- Lots of emotions (with favorable cards, these are very positive emotions, but with negative cards, these are negative emotions)

- All is well - this relationship is in harmony

- Can be a spontaneous connection

- Depending on the question and the surrounding cards, it can also talk about an open relationship

- Without any troubles, the relationship is flowing smoothly and effortlessly

- Expressing one's feelings unselfconsciously and without restraint

DESCRIBING A PERSON:

- Mediterranean looking

- Blue or green eyes

- Darker hair color

- Darker skin tone

- Attractive looking

- Sensitive and compassionate

- An entrepreneur

- A business person

- Convincing

- This person is independent, confident, and competent

- Wants to be free

- Likes to spend money

- Likes to travel

- A smart person

HEALTH AND BODY PART:

- Depending on the context and question, the Fish card can stand for doctors' bills

- Body fluids like, for example, blood, sperm, sweat, urine

- Example: Rider + Fish = diarrhea

- Kidney

- Bladder

- Alcoholism

- Keep hydrated

MONEY:

- Surrounded by positive cards, money will flow to you

- An improvement

- Fulfillment

- A profit

NOTE: The cards that touch the Fish will give insight if it's a gain of money or a loss. If you look at the Fish card alone, it symbolizes prosperity and abundance. The cards next to it color it.

ADVICE:

- Go with the flow

- Let things happen

- Don't control the situation - let it flow

- Listen to your intuition

- Be independent, self-sufficient

- Be generous

OBJECTS:

- A Fish
- Anything that has to do with the subject fish, for example, an aquarium
- Seafood
- A place with a lot of water (in one of my readings, it came up as the laundry room!)
- In a daily draw, it came up as flooding in the basement
- The stock markets
- Anything that has to do with money
- A bar or other places where there is a lot of drinking

TIMING:

- In the early mornings and evenings, and during a full moon and a new moon because this is the best time for fishing
- For me, it will happen once the client changes his/her mindset and lets go and lets it flow; when someone is giving, then abundance will follow

IN A GRAND TABLEAU, IF the Fish card lands in the house of the Fox, that tells me something is wrong with the finances.

IN A GRAND TABLEAU, IF THE FISH CARD IS VERY CLOSE OR CLOSE TO THE SIGNIFICATOR CARD:

The Fish card stands for the financial situation. Having the Fish very close or close to the Significator together with other positive cards means the Man/Woman has a stable and secure financial situation. But if negative cards are around the Fish, that means there are challenges with the finances; obstacles and troubles will follow. Having the Fish in the comfort zone (very close or close to the Significator) indicates prosperous outcomes in all ventures. It predicts great fortune and positive changes - the surrounding cards will give insight into what areas of life are about to prosper. In these positions, together with other favorable cards, the Fish always brings success into one's life. The Fish has the power to increase the effects of the positive and negative cards. Examine if there are any Life Area cards around the Fish; the Fish can bring changes or movement to those areas of life - either positive or negative, depending on the other cards around it. If the Significator is self-employed, the Fish will represent his/her business, and the cards that surround the Fish will give information about the circumstances of that business.

IN A GRAND TABLEAU, IF THE FISH CARD IS FAR OR VERY FAR FROM THE SIGNIFICATOR:

Having the Fish card far or very far means there will be challenges and difficulties when it comes to one's enterprises; one's undertakings will be hard to reach, and projects will fail. The financial situation may be affected very negatively, especially if the Ship (extra profits and revenues) and the Anchor (stability and security) are also far from the Significator. There might be unforeseen expenses coming for the Significator. The surrounding cards will give more information.

Client Examples:

Jane asked: "Will I have money coming in this month?"

Fish + Crossroads + Child =

Answer: "Yes, money will be coming in, but a small amount."

Lucy asked: "Will my unemployment benefits be extended?"

Fish + Scythe + Clouds =

Answer: No, there will be a cut in finances.

Kevin asked: "Will my work project be successful?"

Book + Fish + Coffin =

Answer: No, unfortunately, your project will fail.

Chapter Thirty-Eight

Card #35 - Anchor - 9 of Spades

I'll keep your
Heart anchored
In my soul, for
As long as we
Both shall live

The Anchor card #35 is a **positive** card, but negative cards around the Anchor make it heavy and intensify the negative cards.

- The core meaning of the Anchor is **fortune** and **reaching one's goals**

- The Anchor keeps something in place

- The Anchor brings luck in love; it symbolizes loyalty, trust, dependability, reliability, and security, especially in a relationship context. The Anchor is one of the important relationship cards; together with the Heart and the Ring, it brings stability and faithfulness into the relationship.

- It talks about something long-lasting, safe, and not movable - this applies to all aspects of life

- The Anchor stands for determination and perseverance

- All the attributes of the Anchor are deep-rooted

- The Anchor also talks about reaching one's goals and dropping one's Anchor

- But on the negative side, if the Anchor is surrounded by negative cards, it becomes like a heavy chain pulling and weighing us down, like ball and chain. It keeps us stuck in a situation.

- The Anchor reinforces the attributes of its surrounding cards; it makes something long-lasting. For example, Moon + Anchor = long-lasting romance. Ring + Anchor = lifelong marriage, secure partnership. Bear + Anchor = Secure financial situation. Cross + Anchor = long-term suffering.

- In a yes/no question, the Anchor means yes!

IN A RELATIONSHIP:

- The Anchor is one of my favorite cards to get in a relationship reading because it shows a faithful and committed relationship that is stable and secure.

- A sincere relationship

- Settling down

- You can trust your partner

- This relationship lasts a lifetime

- A strong bond

- Both partners are anchored together

DESCRIBING A PERSON:

- May have bigger, curvy hips, tanned skin tone, and blue-green eye color like the ocean

- If we want to analyze somebody's personality, it might point to stubbornness - the person might be set in his/her ways

- If the Anchor is describing a person, it's a very reliable individual whom you can trust

- Dependable and always there for you if one needs help

- It's a faithful and loyal person

- This individual is stable, secure, and established

- Settled

HEALTH AND BODY PART:

- Hips, pelvis

- In a health reading, the Anchor brings hope - it is a good card to get at the end of a line reading. It points out that the condition is strong and stable, but if there are negative cards around it, then it can refer to an incurable disease. When I did a reading about my mother's illness, I got the Coffin + Anchor, which told me that her condition was incurable - and sadly, it was.

MONEY:

- This is a very good card to get in a money reading because it shows that the financial situation is stable and secure

- Money is growing, for example, like investments

ADVICE:

- Be persistent

- Continue firmly in a course of action despite difficulties

- Be confident and determined

- Don't give up

- You are able to do this if you persist

OBJECTS:

- An Anchor

- Something that looks like an Anchor, for example, a hook

- Anything that has to do with a harbor or pier

- Can represent anything heavy like weights, a heavy chain, something that weighs things down

- An object that is made out of metal

TIMING:

- A lifetime

- It will take a very long time

- It may take several years

IN A GRAND TABLEAU, IF THE ANCHOR IS VERY CLOSE OR CLOSE TO THE SIGNIFICATOR CARD:

If the Anchor is very close or close to the Man/Woman card, that means stability and security in matters of the heart and the finances are present. The Anchor in these positions brings hope. Having the Anchor close symbolizes faithfulness in love. The

Anchor emphasizes the positive aspects of the positive cards; in other words, it reinforces the positive cards.

IN A GRAND TABLEAU, IF THE ANCHOR IS FAR OR VERY FAR FROM THE SIGNIFICATOR:

In these positions, the financial situation might be unstable; to get more information, examine the surrounding cards and look where the Fish and the Ship landed. Hope and security are out of reach for the duration of this spread. The Significator might be thoughtless of one's actions, which may lead to danger or loss. If the Anchor is surrounded by negative cards, challenges will emerge. My mother taught me according to the old instructions: if the Anchor is surrounded by negative cards, it's a bad omen for traveling.

Here is an example of when the Anchor turns negative:

If you get the Whip + Anchor = this could be an argument that doesn't end well or no solution is found. In this example, we see that when the Anchor follows a negative card, it will reinforce the effects of the negative card and keeps them there.

The converse is true: If the Anchor follows a positive card, it reinforces the positive effects of the positive card. For example, Key + Anchor= Success that is certain.

Client Example:

Anchor + Cross = Long-term suffering

This was a daily draw I did for a client:

Stars + Birds + Garden + Dog + Anchor

I told her today she would have lots of online communication with lifelong friends…and she did!

Personal example:

One day, I was laying out a Grand Tableau for a client and noticed that the Heart card was missing from my deck! I was surprised because I had never lost or misplaced something, so I looked in my entire house for that missing card. I searched all evening until 1 am without any luck. I went to bed frustrated.

The next morning, I got the idea to ask my cards where that missing Heart card might be.

Here is what I pulled:

House + Bed + Cross + Anchor

By the way, I used the Rana George Lenormand deck, which contains 4 extra cards, one of them is the BED card #39

When I saw the House card, I knew it was in the house.

The BED card told me it was in my bedroom.

When I saw the CROSS card and the ANCHOR card, I immediately got HEATER! My heater in the bedroom looks like a Cross, and the Anchor made me think stuck under something metal...

I looked under my heater with a flashlight, and there it was- my Heart card! I felt like I had won the lottery! I am always amazed at how precise the Lenormand answers are!

Chapter Thirty-Nine

Card #36 - Cross - 6 of Clubs

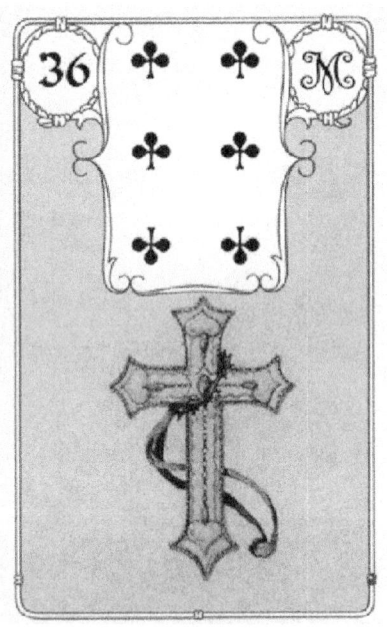

Sometimes the only way
To carry a heavy burden is
To share it with another.
- Jim Butcher -

The Cross card #36 is a **negative** card.

- The core meaning of the Cross is **GRIEF**

- The Cross adds a lot of heaviness to the reading

- The Cross symbolizes burdens, a hard time, and pain

- Hardship and tears will follow

- Misfortune, unhappy events

- Sorrow, suffering

- Despair

- Painful challenges

- Worries and troubles

- Regret and guilt

- Emotional loss, crying

- It can symbolize a test we have to go through to learn a life lesson that makes us grow

- Depending on the context and question, the Cross can also stand for destiny and fate; Karma - what is sent out will come back

- Religion, praying, and a belief

IN A RELATIONSHIP:

- A painful relationship

- Emotional pain

- Lots of sadness because things are not developing as you hoped for

- Challenges

- A separation

- The partner might carry heavy burdens from the past

- An unhappy connection
- The partner is not there for you; he/she let you down
- Depending on the context, the question, and the surrounding cards, the Cross could symbolize a relationship that is destined to be

DESCRIBING A PERSON:

- A tall person, on the slim side
- Can have long arms and legs
- Straight posture
- Exhausted looking
- Tired looking face
- Drained
- Sad face - doesn't smile often
- Reserved personality
- Can be a religious person
- Somebody who complains and worries a lot
- A depressed, negative person
- A person who feels down and unhappy all the time
- A sick person (mentally or physically)

HEALTH AND BODY PART:

- In a health context, the Cross brings pain and suffering
- Setbacks
- Back and shoulders

- Very often, I get the Cross in health readings associated with lower back pain

MONEY:

- Financial burdens
- Money sacrifices
- Bad investments
- Money problems

ADVICE:

- Get help
- Ask for help
- Pray
- Reevaluate your beliefs
- Be really careful what you think about because what you think about expands

OBJECTS:

- A Cross or something that looks like a Cross
- In combination with the Tower, it can stand for a church

TIMING:

- Patience is required; it may take time
- Up to 6 months
- NOTE: If you are unsure how to interpret the timing, pull a clarifying card to get better insight

In a Grand Tableau, the meaning depends on the context, the question, and the surrounding card constellation. For example, in a love reading, if the Man card lands in the house of the Moon and the Cross card is connected, it means that this relationship is destined to be - a karmic relationship (connections that are believed to have been formed across multiple lifetimes, carrying lessons and unresolved issues from the past into the present). Or if the Heart card lands in the house of the Cross, that means this love is your destiny. Good or bad? The surrounding cards and card constellations will give you more insight.

IN A GRAND TABLEAU, IF THE CROSS CARD IS VERY CLOSE OR CLOSE TO THE SIGNIFICATOR:

The Cross brings misfortunes and problems in all areas of life. But if the Cross (just like the Mice card) falls very close or close to the Significator, it predicts that the troubles and challenges are short-lived; the misery won't last long, and the Significator has control over it. Check which Life Area cards (family, career, love, finances) are being affected by the Cross. If the Cross is surrounded by negative cards, it prolongs the sorrow and makes the burdens even heavier. If cards like the Moon and the Heart are in combination with the Cross, it predicts deep emotional pain and suffering inside. On the other hand, if the Cross is surrounded by very positive cards, the suffering won't last long. An interesting thing to look at is which card is underneath the Cross. The card under the Cross is being pinned down by the Cross. For example, if the Ring card is under the Cross, we can say that the relationship is very burdened and is suffering. The surrounding cards will give more insight. The card underneath the Cross is being stabbed. This means the card being stabbed is heavily burdened or has problems.

My Mother taught me that if the Cross appears as the very first card in a Grand Tableau (in the house of the Rider), it predicts deep sorrow. If in this spread, the Significator is far away from cards like Heart, Ring, Anchor, Child, Garden, and Dog (the love and friendship cards), it indicates that the sadness, the grief, and the burdens will last a very long time and can be healed only through love.

IN A GRAND TABLEAU, IF THE CROSS IS FAR OR VERY FAR FROM THE SIGNIFICATOR CARD:

If the Cross card lands far away from the Significator, that means the Man/Woman does not have much control over the troubles and difficulties. It will take a much longer time to overcome those challenges and the suffering. Also, it is best to have the Cross in the spread under the Significator card (and best would be if it lands very close or close), which will give the Man/Woman more control over the problem. The Cross always influences the cards it touches negatively. But positive cards lessen the negative impact of the Cross.

Also, pay attention to which house of the Grand Tableau the Cross has landed in. It will give you insight into where the troubles are coming from. For example, if the Cross lands in the house of the Child, that means there are challenges with one's children. Or if the Cross lands in the house of the House, that indicates there are troubles and difficulties with one's family or family matters.

Card Combination Examples:

Cross + Anchor = Long term suffering

Cross + Ship = A troubled journey

Cross + Birds = Heavy, negative conversations

Cross + Scythe = Severe pain

Cross + Mountain = Being overburdened

Cross + Tower = Church

Cross + Moon = Depression, having a very hard time

Cross + Key = An important life lesson that leads to success

Client Example:

Here is a story from my client Lucy: Lucy asked me how her work meeting would go.

Three cards flew out of the deck. When that happens, I know these are the important cards from which to receive the message.

Birds + Mice + Cross

My answer was her meeting would be very stressful and burdensome.

She later confirmed that it was indeed very unpleasant.

Birds # 12 = Conversations

Mice # 23 = Stress, Anxiety

Cross # 36 = Burdens, hard time

Personal Example:

Here is a very personal story about my mother from me. The day my mother passed away, I got the following in my daily draw: Tower + Coffin + Cross

When I saw these cards, I had a feeling that she would pass today. The Tower represents the hospital, and the Coffin + Cross combination talks about pain, sadness, and grief. I didn't want to believe it, and I took a different deck and shuffled again. Two cards flew out of the deck: Heart + Cross. This combination talks about very painful feelings. I was angry at the cards, took another deck, and shuffled again… I pulled Moon + Cross. This combination is similar to the Heart + Cross combo; it predicts emotional pain and sadness. A couple of hours later, my mother passed. Today, I know she didn't pass anywhere, but rather, she transitioned into another dimension and is still around to connect with and guide me.

I am always amazed at how precise the cards can be! After she passed that day, I pulled some more cards for myself, and I got:

Garden + Heart + Dog + Child + Anchor = This combination told me I would receive loving support from my very close friends (Garden, Dog, and Child are the friendship cards). Indeed, I would not be able to handle this situation without my supporting lifelong friends, who are represented by the Anchor card at the end.

Chapter Forty
How to Ask a Yes/No Question

P ositive cards are a yes! Negative cards are a no!

While shuffling the cards, you have to tell your cards if you want a yes/no answer or if you want to see a prediction.

For a yes/no question, the 3 card spread or the 5 card spread are best. The last card always represents the answer. If you choose the 3 card spread, the card in the middle is the focus card; it stands for the situation and the other two cards describe it.

Example: Will Peter propose to Jane?
Birds + Bouquet + Ring

In this example we see there will be communication (Birds # 12). The bouquet (card # 9) can be a surprise, and the last card, the ring (card # 25), is our answer, which is a yes.

If you choose the 5 card spread, then the first 2 cards will affirm the context, the card in the middle is our focus card, and the last 2 cards represent the outcome (especially the 5th card).

Example: Will John get the promotion?
Clouds + Mice + Scythe + Sun + Key

In this example, the first two cards show John's doubts (Cloud card # 6) and anxiety (Mice card # 23), but they will be cleared away, and a decision will be made (Scythe card # 10). The last two cards are our answer, which is a definite yes (Sun card # 31 and Key card # 33).

If you want to predict timing, you have to tell your cards while you're shuffling them that the very last card in a line reading will be your answer. It's important to stick to one system because there are so many readers out there, and everybody has their own system. You have to do what works best for you!

Here is an example of a predictive reading:

My client Loren purchased a self-study online course and asked me if she would pass the exam in 6 months.

I drew: Lilies + Fox + Stars + Child + Crossroads

Immediately, I could tell that Lauren would not finish this course because the Lilies + Fox say that something is wrong (e.g., lies), and the Stars + Child + Crossroads combination indicates a new path/going a different way.

It turns out that Lauren had decided to drop out and not participate in this course. In order to get her money back, she lied...(Lilies + Fox = not being honest).

Chapter Forty-One
The Line Reading

Throughout the book, when I described every card in detail, I gave you examples of readings using a short line of cards, either 3, 5, or 7 cards. This line of cards is used for a quick answer. You can use a line of 3 or, in other words, a 3-card spread for a quick yes/no answer or a 5-card spread for more details. To get more information about a matter, I would do a line of 7 (a 7-card spread). The card in the middle is the Focus card or the situation, and the other two cards next to the Focus card describe the situation. No matter what spread you choose, the last card is the answer card or the outcome.

Here is an example of a line of 5 (a 5-card spread):

Marc asked me: "What was the reason I didn't get the job?" I pulled:

LETTER + LILIES + BOOK + MICE + TOWER

In the middle, we have the BOOK card as the focus card, the Book as the subject, and the other cards describe the subject.

When I saw this line, I knew Marc didn't get this job because he lacked a certain certification. The Lilies card in this line stands for the experience needed for this position. The Lilies card is mirroring the Mice card on the other side, which tells me Marc lacks some experience. The Book in the middle with the Mice next to it tells me Marc lacks the certification needed to get this higher position (Tower).

Marc's feedback: Mark received an email from the interviewing company saying that they would like to hire him, but only if he's willing to get certified in a specific field.

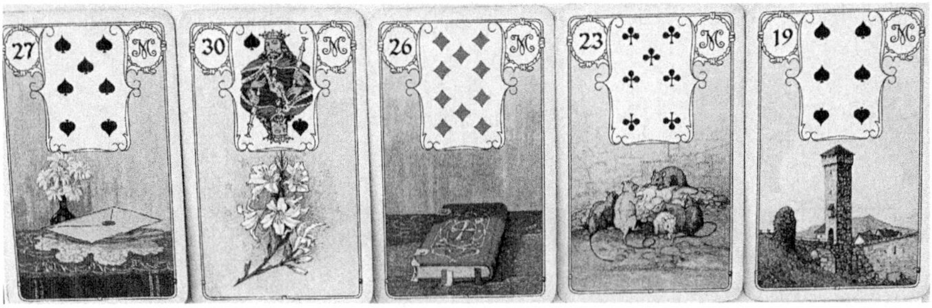
27
30
26
23
19

Chapter Forty-Two
THE BOX SPREAD

Now, I am going to introduce you to the Box Spread. A Box Spread consists of 9 cards in a 3x3 layout. This was a real reading I did for my client Sam, who wanted to relocate overseas but had many financial obstacles.

Sam's question was: "Will I be able to do this move within the next 3 months?"

230 SYLVIA KA'UHANE

Using the following for rules interpretation:

- Past = cards 7, 2, 6

- Present = cards 3, 1, 5

- Future = cards 8, 4, 9

- Answer = card #9

- Focus card = card #1

Using the following for rules interpretation:

- What's on somebody's mind (the worries, concerns) = 7, 3, 8

- What somebody is dealing with at the moment = 2, 1, 4

- What is under control (known facts) = 6, 5, 9

- Indirect influences (The X-diagonals) show us the subject and the atmosphere of the reading = 7, 1, 9 and 8, 1, 6

- Energy or the topic (The 4 corners) = 7, 8, 6, 9

- Some extra information, like a confirmation (the 4 cards that surround the Focus card like a bow) = 2, 3, 4, 5

NOTE: Some readers preselect a Focus card, but I never preselect a Focus card; I let the cards choose the Focus card!

232 SYLVIA KA'UHANE

Here are the card positions from 1 to 9. I lay them down clockwise, but if you like, you can choose your own as long as you stick to one method.

So, let's start to take the BOX Spread apart!

Cards number 7, 2, and 6 stand for the past.

We have the Mountain + Coffin + Key

We see Sam has had many obstacles and delays in the past, and there was an ending that led to a solution. It was a good ending for Sam because we have the Key card.

The Coffin + Key combination tells us a solution is found, and there will be an end to misfortune.

The Coffin + Child combination shows us clearly something will end and something new is going to start.

The Mountain + Coffin combination shows us that the difficult times will end.

Sam's feedback: He had lots of financial obstacles in the past (Mountain), but then he got a new position offered overseas, which is going to give him more money (Key). So, Sam quit his job (Coffin) but wasn't sure if he could handle this move because of his current finances.

Cards number 3, 1, and 5 stand for the present.

We have Scythe + Stork + Child.

The Scythe shows the ending, which leads to a sudden and fast change (Scythe + Stork) and something new, a new start, or a new change, starting at the beginning (Stork + Child).

Cards number 8, 4, and 9 stand for the future.

We have Crossroads, House, and Ship.

Here we see Sam will have to make a decision regarding a house or family; with the Crossroads, it can talk about two houses.

The House + Ship combination clearly predicts that Sam will make that move overseas.

Sam's feedback after 3 months:

He managed financially to make that move, but he had to decide whether to keep his home in the USA for now or let it go. The result was that Sam rented his place in the USA out and moved overseas to start his new job.

Card numbers 7, 3, and 8 stand for what is on Sam's mind. His worries and concerns:

We have Mountain, Scythe, and Crossroads.

Here, we see what is weighing heavily on Sam's mind: Obstacles (Mountain) lead to delays, and Sam knows he has to make a fast decision (Scythe + Crossroads) regarding this matter.

The Mountain + Scythe combination talks about a dead end. But he knows it is still possible to conquer these obstacles (Mountain + Scythe = Obstacles are removed/cleared).

Cards 2, 1, and 4 stand for what Sam is dealing with at the moment:

We have Coffin, Stork, and House.

Coffin + Stork = always means a big change in somebody's life, and it also indicates moving house.

The Stork + House combination also predicts a change of residence. As we know now, Sam quit his job and was making plans to move overseas to start a new position. The cards keep repeating to show the upcoming move.

Cards 6, 5, and 9 stand for what Sam has under control / what is known to him:

We have Key, Child, and Ship.

The Key + Child combination indicates a promising new beginning, and the Child + Ship combination shows us a new movement. As we know, Sam got a new job offered overseas, which requires him to relocate.

Cards 7, 1, 9, and 8, 1, 6 show us the subject and the atmosphere of the reading:

We have Mountain + Stork + Ship and Crossroads + Stork + Key.

The Mountain + Stork combination shows us that Sam is going to overcome these obstacles, and Stork + Ship tells us that Sam is going to move overseas. As you can see, this Box Spread is repeating the upcoming move over and over.

The cards 7, 8, 6, and 9 (4 corners) show us the energy of this spread/topic:

We have Mountain + Crossroads + Key + Ship

The 4 corners of this Box spread show us the difficult decision Sam has to make, but it also shows there will be solutions found and that Sam's move will be a success.

The cards in positions 2, 3, 4, and 5 (the cards that surround the Focus card like a bow or a diamond) give us some extra information:

We have Coffin + Scythe + House + Child.

In this card combination, we see that there will be a sudden ending (Coffin), a sudden change in residence (Scythe + House), and a new home (House + Child).

The card that lands in the number 9 position is the outcome:

Here we have the Ship card which shows us clearly the trip.

Chapter Forty-Three

Tips on How to Read a Grand Tableau

Before I start a Lenormand card reading, I center myself by doing a short meditation to clear my mind.

I relax and then choose a card deck I really feel connected to.

Most of the time, I'd like to use the Rana George Lenormand cards because they have four extra cards, which I love, especially the Market #40, which represents the work card to free the Fox #14 from the work topic, and the Bed card #39, which I use as the sex card to free the Whip card from the sex topic.

I shuffle the cards and thank my spirit guides for removing all negative energies from them and for removing the energies from my past readings. I thank my spirit guides for blessing every single card, and I give thanks so that I can help people with my card readings. I do this ritual before and after a reading.

Then, I shuffle the cards and concentrate on my client's question (only one question at a time!) I charge/activate the cards that need to be charged. In other words, I put my intention on one specific card to represent a certain person or matter. For example, my client Lisa is represented by card #29, the Woman card; her husband is represented by card #28, the Man card; her child is represented by the Child card #13; her boss is represented by the Bear card #15. If, for example, there is a third party involved, then I charge the Dog card to represent that person.

When I shuffle the cards, I shuffle until one falls out or flips or turns face up by itself, or one card stops me from shuffling – I call those cards the stoppers! Then I know which cards to pick because they look like they want to jump out of the deck. The clearest answers I get are from those cards that fly out of the deck while shuffling. In the end, I always thank my spirit guides for the answers.

Always remember to be in a good state of mind when you perform a card reading. Also, don't panic when the prediction looks very negative.

The cards predict your future based on your current energy, but if you change that energy, that prediction will also change! In other words: "YOU CREATE YOUR OWN REALITY!" (Dyer, W.W., Change Your Thoughts - Change Your Life: Living the Wisdom of the Tao, 2009). What you think you create!

The Grand Tableau, also called "the big picture," where all 36 cards are on the table, is the biggest spread of the Lenormand. It shows the Significator's life in a certain time frame you chose, for example, 3 months or 6 months. You can use any time frame you want as long as you tell your cards while you are shuffling. In other words, put your intention of a time frame in your mind: "Please, spirit guides, give me insight about my client's (Name of client) life within the next 3 months".

Also, while you are shuffling the cards, assign the person cards to the characters involved in this reading. That way, you know who is who. This is why I ask my client before we start the reading about which people my client wants to know about. This way, I can assign the characters.

The Grand Tableau answers many questions in a single spread. You see all the Life Area cards and what the circumstances are in each of these areas.

There are two techniques to lay a Grand Tableau: The 4x8+4 spread and the 9x4 spread.

The 4x8+4 spread resonates with me the most because the last 4 cards on the bottom are, for me, very important to predict an outcome. You have to tell your cards while you are shuffling and before laying out the cards on the table what the last 4 cards represent. I tell my deck the last 4 cards are the outcome line - the answer line or I also see it as the line of destiny.

First, I locate the two Significator cards (Man + Woman). Like I described earlier in the chapter of both Significators (#28 + #29) I look where they landed. On top or the bottom? That will give me insight if the Significator is in control of the situation or not. Is the Man/Woman in the 8th column of the Grand Tableau or the 1st column? That shows me if the Significator is ending or starting a new chapter of his/her life. If the Significator landed in the middle of the spread, that shows me a lot is going on in the Significator's life.

You can reread the chapter about the two Significator cards, where I explain the position of the Man/Woman card in detail.

After locating the two Significator cards, I look at the first 3 cards of the Grand Tableau. The first 3 cards show me the topic of the reading:

THE LENORMAND

For example, here we have Mice + Ring + Dog

This was a reading for a client who had stress and worries in her relationship, and at the same time, she met a new man, represented by the Dog. Seeing that, I knew this Grand Tableau was about her relationship and the new man she met.

After knowing what the subject of the Grand Tableau is, I look at the 4 corners:

1 Rider	2 Clover	3 Ship	4 House	5 Tree	6 Clouds	7 Snake	8 Coffin
9 Bouquet	10 Scythe	11 Whip	12 Birds	13 Child	14 Fox	15 Bear	16 Star
17 Stork	18 Dog	19 Tower	20 Garden	21 Mountain	22 Crossroad	23 Mice	24 Heart
25 Ring	26 Book	27 Letter	28 Man	29 Woman	30 Lily	31 Sun	32 Moon
		33 Key	34 Fish	35 Anchor	36 Cross		

The 4 corners will give us an idea of why the client asked this question.

Here, for example, we have the Mice in the upper left corner and the Book in the upper right corner, and in the lower right corner, we see the Scythe, and in the lower left corner, we have the fish.

So, that shows me my client has a lot of anxiety and worries that when her secret is revealed, her finances will be cut.

Then I asked my client if she was hiding something and was worried that if it came out, the money flow would be cut?

My client confirmed that her Ex supports her financially and still wants her to return to him, but at the same time, she met a new man. Now, she is very worried that if her Ex finds out she is seeing somebody new, he might stop supporting her financially.

MIRRORING TECHNIQUE:

Mirroring means that if we divide the Grand Tableau into 2 parts, there is always a card in the same position on the other side - vertical and horizontal. Here is an example:

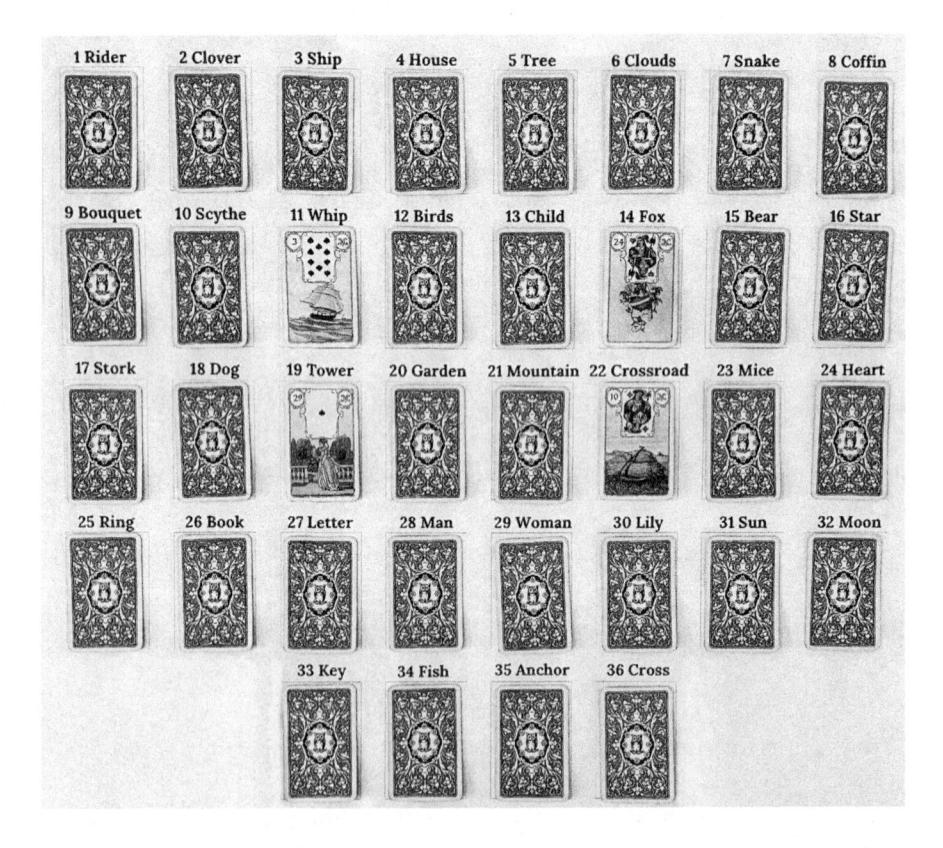

1 Rider	2 Clover	3 Ship	4 House	5 Tree	6 Clouds	7 Snake	8 Coffin
9 Bouquet	10 Scythe	11 Whip	12 Birds	13 Child	14 Fox	15 Bear	16 Star
17 Stork	18 Dog	19 Tower	20 Garden	21 Mountain	22 Crossroad	23 Mice	24 Heart
25 Ring	26 Book	27 Letter	28 Man	29 Woman	30 Lily	31 Sun	32 Moon
		33 Key	34 Fish	35 Anchor	36 Cross		

NOTE: The last 4 cards on the bottom of a 4x8+4 spread are not used for mirroring!

In this example above, we see the Ship mirrors with the Heart and the Woman mirrors with the Scythe. In this scenario, it meant that the Woman (my client) was emotionally hurt and lost her feelings for the man she was asking about. The Ship in this example shows us that love is at a distance.

When I describe every single card, I talk about **very close** and **close** to the Significator, and I talk about **far** and **very far** from the Significator.

1 Rider	2 Clover	3 Ship	4 House	5 Tree	6 Clouds	7 Snake	8 Coffin
9 Bouquet	10 Scythe	11 Whip	12 Birds	13 Child	14 Fox	15 Bear	16 Star
17 Stork	18 Dog	19 Tower	20 Garden	21 Mountain	22 Crossroad	23 Mice	24 Heart
				B	S	A	
25 Ring	26 Book	27 Letter	28 Man	29 Woman	30 Lily	31 Sun	32 Moon
		B	A	A	A	B	
		33 Key	34 Fish	35 Anchor	36 Cross		
		B	B	B	B		

S = Significator

The cards that are very close to the Significator are touching the Man/Woman card. The cards that are close to the Significator are touching the very close cards. The cards that are far from the Significator are touching the close cards. The very far cards are touching the far cards. Here is an example:

- The A cards are the very close cards; they are touching the Significator directly.

- The B cards are the ones that are close; they are touching the very close cards.

- The C cards are the far cards; they are touching the close cards.

- The D cards are the very far cards; they are touching the far cards.

KNIGHTING:

The Knighting technique comes from chess. The starting point is the Significator card (S) or any Life Area card (for example, Ring for relationships), and you would like to get more insight into the circumstances. We move two cards forward and then left and right (like an L-shape or a "Knight's move" away from it). The Knighting technique goes in either direction (either horizontally or vertically) and then one position perpendicular to that direction. The cards that are a Knight's move away from the Significator or Life Area cards are considered to be "Knighted" by it. The Knighted cards are then interpreted in relation to the Significator or Life Area cards, suggesting themes, influences, or outcomes connected to the Significator or Life Area cards' primary significance. Here is an example:

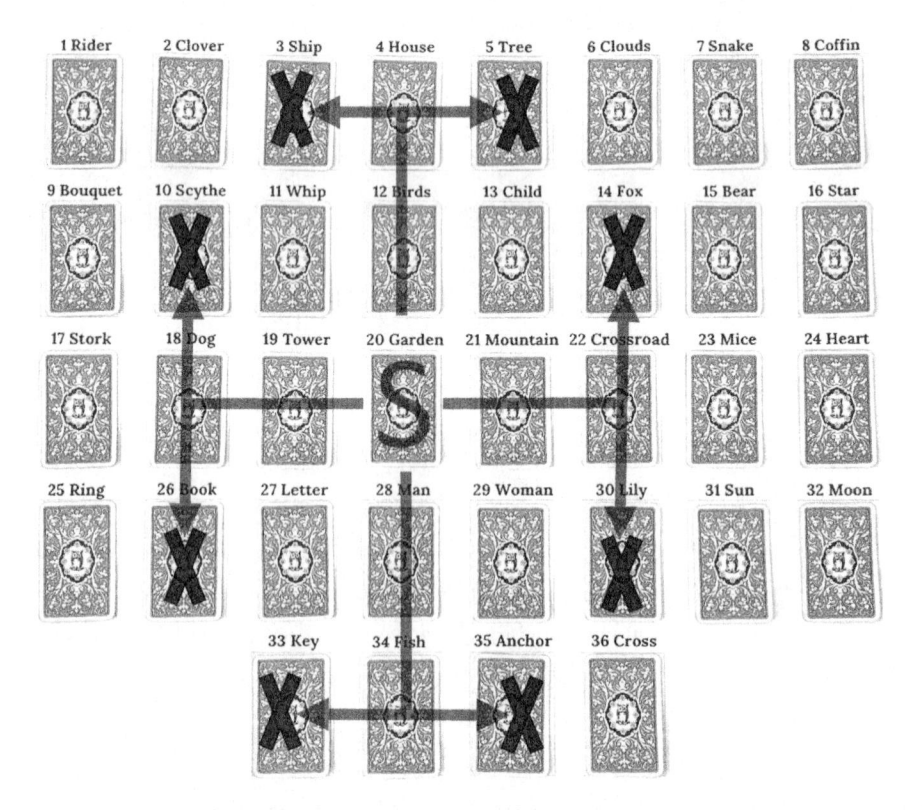

CHOOSING A TIME FRAME:

The most common time frame in a Grand Tableau is the Past - Present and Future spread: The cards to the left of the Significator represent the past. The cards on top and below the Significator stand for the present, and the cards to the right of the Significator represent the future.

My clients are not interested in what happened in the past. So, while I'm shuffling the cards, I tell my deck I want the entire Grand Tableau to represent only the future! So, I am working with only one time frame. In that case, the cards that fall to the left of the person card will stand for the future and not the past.

Now, if your client wishes, you can do the same thing for only the past. Then, I would tell my cards while I'm shuffling to show me only the past with no future.

Now, let's say you are working with the most common Grand Tableau spread: The Past-Present-Future spread. The diagonals starting from the Significator card (S) stand also for a specific time frame:

- The F line of cards in the upper right = What will happen very soon in the future
- The G line of cards lower right = What happens later in the future
- The C line of cards in the upper left = Events that happened close to now
- The D line of cards lower left = Further away from the past
- B line of cards = Past
- E line of cards = Future
- A line of cards = Present

As I mentioned in the Stork chapter, my clients usually prefer a Grand Tableau for 6 months. This is how you calculate the timing in a Grand Tableau:

- I count 2 vertical columns as a month and a half, 4 columns as 3 months, 6 columns as 4.5 months, and 8 columns as 6 months.

- If I do a Grand Tableau for 3 months (12 weeks), then 4 vertical columns represent a month and a half (1.5 months = 6 weeks), and 2 columns are 3 weeks.

NOTE: If you do the Past-Present-Future Grand Tableau, it doesn't matter which way the Significator card is facing. In other words, it doesn't matter which way the character on the card is facing: The right side of the Significator is always the future, and the left side is always the past.

NOTE: Please reread the chapter on both Significator cards (#'s 28 + 29). I described in detail the position the Man/Woman landed in (i.e., Did the Significator land in the First or Last column? On top or bottom?)

THE LENORMAND HOUSES

When you lay out all 36 cards from 1 to 36 in numerical order, these are called the Lenormand houses. "Landing in a house" refers to the placement of a card in a specific position within the spread.

Here is an example of how it looks:

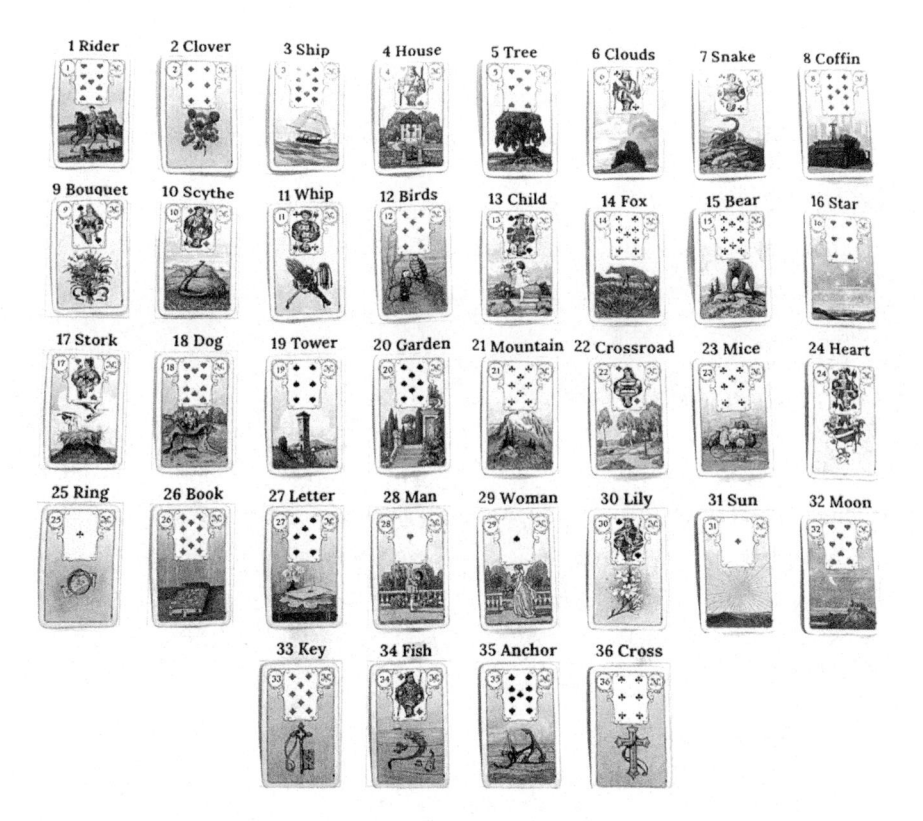

1 Rider	2 Clover	3 Ship	4 House	5 Tree	6 Clouds	7 Snake	8 Coffin
9 Bouquet	10 Scythe	11 Whip	12 Birds	13 Child	14 Fox	15 Bear	16 Star
17 Stork	18 Dog	19 Tower	20 Garden	21 Mountain	22 Crossroad	23 Mice	24 Heart
25 Ring	26 Book	27 Letter	28 Man	29 Woman	30 Lily	31 Sun	32 Moon
		33 Key	34 Fish	35 Anchor	36 Cross		

Note: A "house" is a specific position in the 36-card layout of the Grand Tableau. Each of the 36 positions in the Grand Tableau corresponds to one of the 36 Lenormand cards; these positions are "houses" that carry the essence of the card associated with that number in the sequence of the deck.

The card that lands in a particular house is colored (emotionally) by that house. For example, if the Mountain card lands in the house of the Garden, it indicates an isolation from the social circle going on. The houses are used to follow the "chain of houses". You start with the card you need more information on. For example, if the Significator lands in the house of the Mice, it means the Man/Woman is very stressed and worried. Then you would follow the chain of houses and look where the Mice card landed... If the Mice card landed in the house of the House, that shows us the stress and worries the Significator has come from the family/private life. Now, you would look in which house the House card landed...You continue following the chain of houses until you end up with the card you started.

If a card lands in its own house, it emphasizes its meaning. For example, if the Fox card lands in its own house (the house of the Fox, the 14th position), it amplifies the Fox meaning and urges us to examine the surrounding cards it touches carefully.

The same happens if two cards occupy each other's houses. For example, the Mice card is in the house of the Ring (25th position), and the Ring is in the house of the Mice (23rd position), which shows us there is a lot of stress in the relationship or even a separation or breakup.

WHAT QUESTION TO ASK

You don't need to ask a specific question when you do a Grand Tableau. While you are shuffling, you tell your cards, for example: "Please give me insight about (client's name) life within the next 3 months." Then, when the Grand Tableau is on the table, you examine what's around each Life Area Cards.

Life Area Cards:

- **Tree** = Health
- **Heart** = Love
- **Ring** = Relationships
- **House** = Family, Private life
- **Dog** = Friends or a partner
- **Fox** or **Market** (#40 from the Rana George Lenormand) = Work

- **Child** = Children

- **Ship** = Travel

- **Book** = Study, school, a project

- **Garden** = Social circle, environment

- **Fish** = Money flow, receiving money

- **Bear** = All financial matters

For example, if your client wants to know about their health, you would look at which cards are touching the Tree card. If you want to find out about the circumstances of their finances, you look around the Bear card.

Now, if you do have a specific question, you can ask that one question and then look in the Grand Tableau where that Life Area card that relates to your question landed and read the cards around it like a Box spread. In this case, you don't need to read every single card in the Grand Tableau. Another example is if the client wants to know only about their love life, you read the cards touching the Ring and the Heart and look where the Anchor landed.

THE LAST 4 CARDS IN A GRAND TABLEAU

The last 4 cards of the Grand Tableau can represent an answer to a specific question, an outcome, or the advice that spirit wants to give you. But you have to make it very clear while you are shuffling what these last 4 cards are representing in your reading.

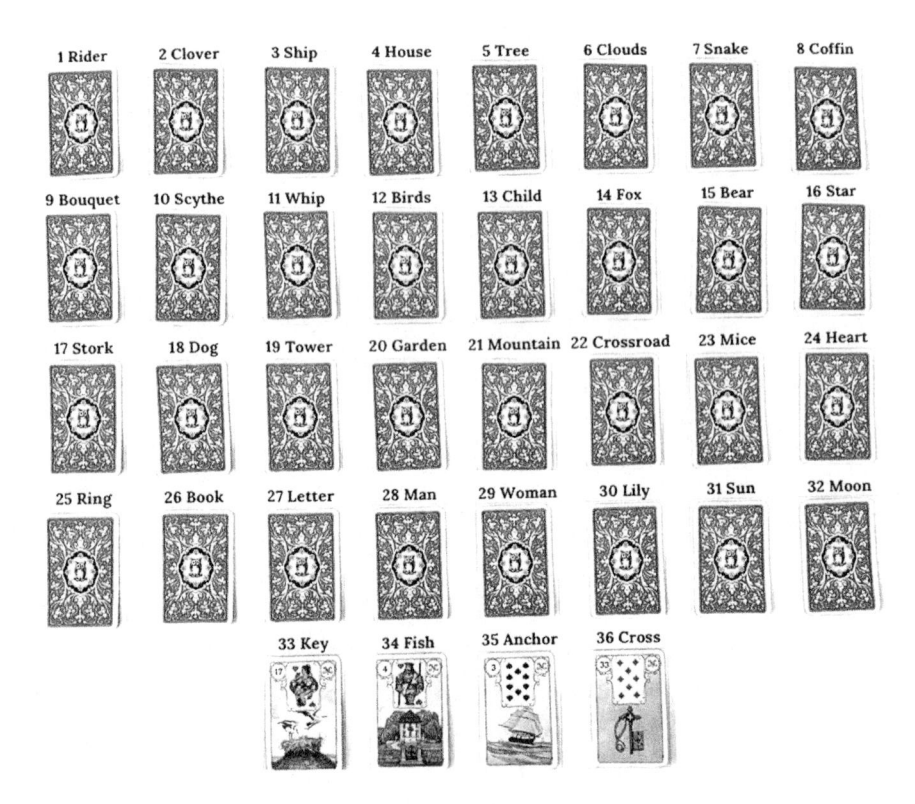

1 Rider	2 Clover	3 Ship	4 House	5 Tree	6 Clouds	7 Snake	8 Coffin
9 Bouquet	10 Scythe	11 Whip	12 Birds	13 Child	14 Fox	15 Bear	16 Star
17 Stork	18 Dog	19 Tower	20 Garden	21 Mountain	22 Crossroad	23 Mice	24 Heart
25 Ring	26 Book	27 Letter	28 Man	29 Woman	30 Lily	31 Sun	32 Moon
		33 Key	34 Fish	35 Anchor	36 Cross		

In the example above, I asked my cards if client Linda was going to move within the next 3 months. I told my cards to show me the answer with the last 4 cards.

Here we have the Stork + House + Ship + Key

This card combination is a definite yes answer. Linda will make that move within the next 3 months, and indeed, she moved.

THE MEETING POINTS OF BOTH SIGNIFICATOR CARDS

Another thing I look at right away when the Grand Tableau is on the table is the meeting points of both Significators, in other words, where the Man and Woman cards intersect. Here is an example:

THE LENORMAND

Like in the picture above, you draw a line from the Man and Woman card until they meet at a certain card.

Here, in this example, we see the Man and Woman are meeting at the Heart + Coffin card. So that shows us it's a very troubled love relationship or the love came to an end. The surrounding cards will give more info, especially the placement of the 3 relationship cards (Ring, Heart, and Anchor). Of course, this technique doesn't work if both Significators are in the same line, either horizontal or vertical.

Chapter Forty-Four
A Real Reading Using the Grand Tableau

F irst, let me explain the characters in this Grand Tableau:

- The Woman card #29 is Carla, my client

- The Bear card #15 is Carla's husband, Paul

- The Man card #28 is Carla's boyfriend, Dan

- The Dog card #18 is Dan's new love interest (3rd party)

THE LENORMAND

The time frame of the Grand Tableau is 3 months, and I told my spirit guides to show me only the future for Carla. Carla's question was about her love life and whether Dan was going to ask Carla to move in with him. Carla planned to divorce her husband. But she couldn't figure out why her boyfriend was hesitating. So, she came to me and asked for a reading.

The very first thing I've noticed is the first 3 cards of the Grand Tableau:

Crossroads + Clouds + Woman. The dark side of the Clouds is facing Carla. This is a very unfavorable card combination. It predicts stormy weather on one's path. Things will not go as planned. Also, the Clouds are in the house of the Clover, and the Clover card landed in the house of the Ring. The Ring card landed in the house of the Cross. This showed me it has to do with her relationship, which is burdened.

Carla (Woman card #29) landed in the house of the Ship (which means a change), and the Ship card landed in the house of the Stork (meaning more change). The Stork card landed in front of her boyfriend, Dan. This chain shows me a change is coming for Carla, and it has to do with Dan, the boyfriend.

Then, I looked for the 3 relationship cards. The Heart landed very far from Carla, and the Heart landed in the house of the Coffin. The Coffin card landed next to the Heart. This shows many problems in the relationship, which may lead to a temporary separation. I say temporary because the Coffin landed before the Heart. Coffin + Heart = love can be rekindled, especially having the Key card under the Coffin.

The second relationship card I look for is the Ring, which also landed very far from Carla and landed in the Cross. That means this relationship is burdened, and Carla needs to learn a lesson.

The Anchor is the third relationship card, which landed very close to Carla and her husband, Paul. Paul is faithful to Carla, and she has a safe and secure life with him.

The husband, Paul, represented by the Bear card, landed in the house of the Whip, and the Whip card landed in Carla's own house, which indicates that Carla will have arguments with her husband, Paul. Carla confirmed this a couple of weeks later, saying that she had many arguments with her husband. Also, we see the Mountain card right in front of Carla, a big obstacle, and what was very interesting is that the Mountain card landed in the house of the House, and the House card landed in the house of the Mountain (these 2 cards mirror each other by occupying each other's houses - so pay extra attention to that message the cards want to convey). That's why I knew the obstacles would be in her home life/family. And indeed, Carla confirmed this later on.

Next, we look at the 4 corners: Crossroads + Heart + Stork + Clover

Whenever I get Crossroads + Heart, it means there are conflicting emotions, and there will be changes in her love life. She needs to make a decision regarding her relationship.

Now, let's look at where Carla and her boyfriend, Dan, intersect.

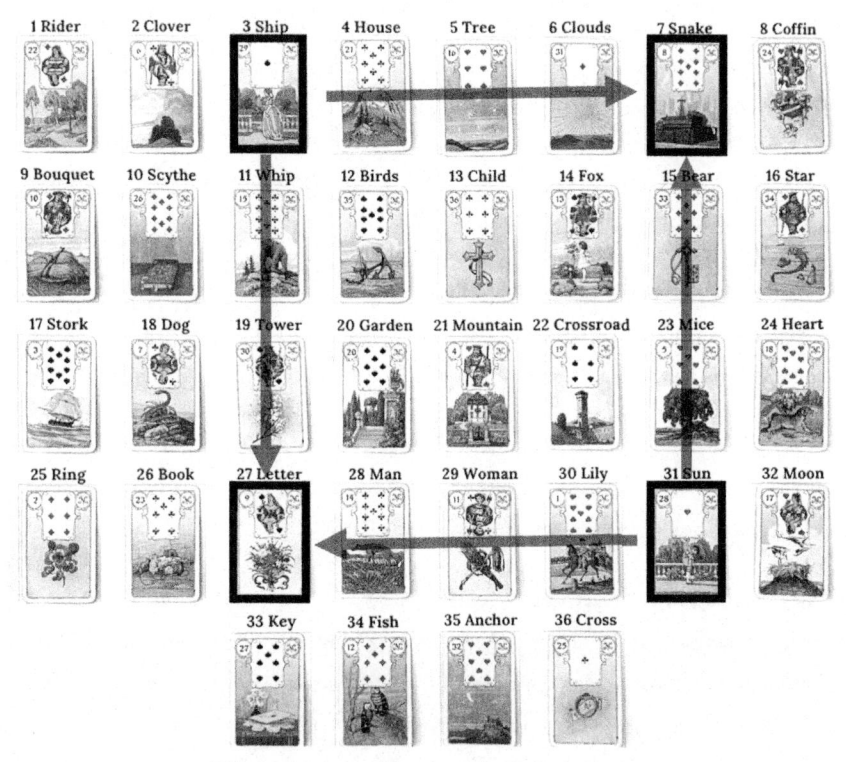

THE LENORMAND

1 Rider	2 Clover	3 Ship	4 House	5 Tree	6 Clouds	7 Snake	8 Coffin
9 Bouquet	10 Scythe	11 Whip	12 Birds	13 Child	14 Fox	15 Bear	16 Star
17 Stork	18 Dog	19 Tower	20 Garden	21 Mountain	22 Crossroad	23 Mice	24 Heart
25 Ring	26 Book	27 Letter	28 Man	29 Woman	30 Lily	31 Sun	32 Moon
			33 Key	34 Fish	35 Anchor	36 Cross	

Where Carla and her boyfriend, Dan, intersect.

Here, we see the meeting points of cards 28 + 29 are the Bouquet and the Coffin, which means there will be disappointments and a very unpleasant surprise.

Remember Carla's question about her boyfriend Dan...she was suspicious that something was going on...so I looked under the Book card to see what the secret was that Dan is hiding from Carla... We see under the Book card is the Snake in the house of the Dog, so that shows us the lies and betrayal and a third-party.

Carla's feedback after 3 months: She discovered that Dan, her boyfriend, has a new love interest.

Another thing that caught my eye is that the Garden card landed in its own house, so we must examine the cards around the Garden carefully. When a card lands in its own house, it's highlighted. So, I knew it had to do with Carla's social circle.

Let's see which cards are around the Garden.

We have three negative cards around the Garden: the Fox, the Whip, and the Cross.

We see underneath the Garden card is the Fox, and the Fox stands for wrongness in this context. The Fox landed in the house of the Man (Carla's boyfriend, Dan), so there's something wrong with that connection. Also, the Fox is connected with the Lilies card, which means something untrustworthy is going on.

The Whip is connected to the Garden, House, and Fox. Carla had many arguments and disagreements in her home life with her Husband Paul (The Bear) and her boyfriend (because the Fox landed in house #28 (Man)).

The Cross card is touching the Garden, which means there will be heavy burdens in her social life. The Cross card is pinning down the House card - another confirmation that Carla's home life will have a heavy atmosphere.

In Carla's vertical line (underneath Carla), we have the Bear (Paul) and the Lilies. Carla has the Lilies underneath her, which shows she is not faithful to her husband, Paul (Bear). Also, the Lilies card touches the Snake and the Mice, which indicates her disloyalty, and this situation is eating away at her peacefulness.

Very close to Carla, we find the Book card, which landed in the house of the Scythe, and the Scythe card is next to the Book. This combination shows me a secret will be revealed. Carla will find out something. Another clue that the secret will be discovered is that in the house of the Book, we find the Mice card, which tells me a secret will be slowly discovered.

In front of Carla, we have the Mountain + Stars, which showed me Carla is losing faith. Mountain + Cross predicts burdens, troubles, and hardship. Mountain + Anchor talks about a long-term blockage.

Although Carla has challenging cards around her, she landed on the top of the Grand Tableau, which means she has control over the situation no matter how bad it is.

Now, let's use the Knighting technique for Carla. We start from the card in position #29, jump two cards to the left and one down, and get: The Scythe.

Now, again, from card 29, we jump two cards to the right and one down, and we get The Cross.

So, we read those two cards together: Scythe + Cross = Painful burdens for Carla, and something will change in her belief system.

Ok, let's move on to the next Knighting round from card 29 starting from below: Two cards down and then left and right.

We get: Snake + Garden = there will be disappointment and sadness from her social circle.

In the picture below, you see the Knighting technique:

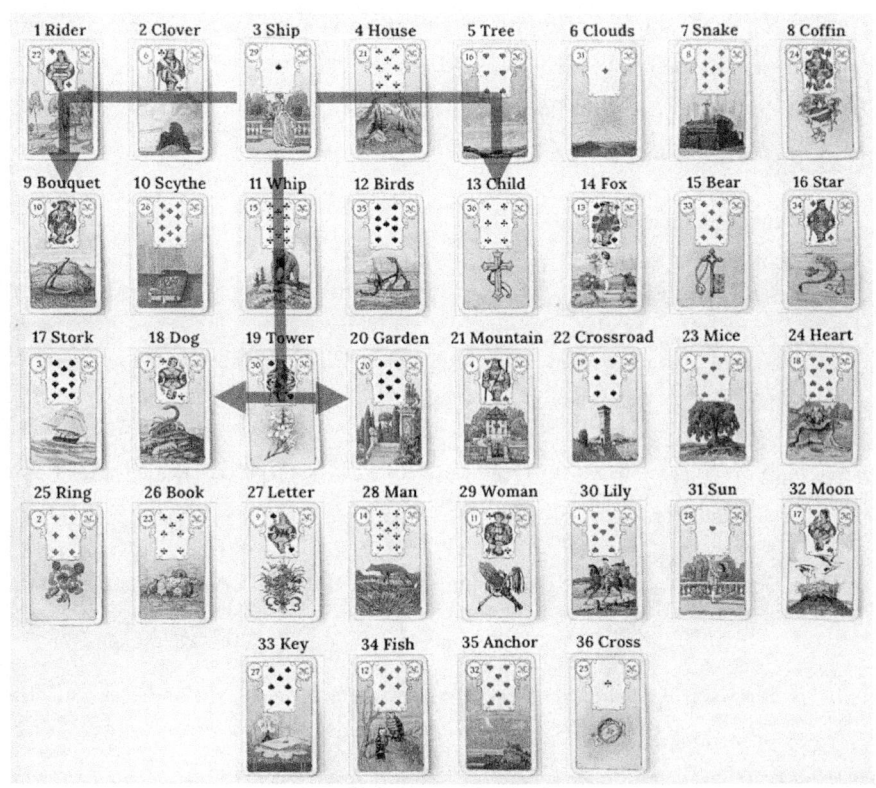

The Knighting Technique

Ok, let's continue with Carla's boyfriend, Dan, who is represented by the Man card #28. Dan landed on the bottom of the Grand Tableau, which indicates that the entire Grand Tableau is weighing heavily over his head. Dan has a lot of pressure on him. Let's follow the chain of houses starting from Dan card 28. Dan landed in the house of the Sun, and the Sun card landed in the house of the Clouds. The Clouds card landed next to Carla in the house of the Clover. So, whenever the Clouds are involved, there will be a lot of confusion. Having the Sun in the house of the Clouds tells me there will be an unexpected troubled situation, and the Clouds card in the house of the Clover predicts misfortune and troubles. I don't follow the entire chain of houses, meaning I stop once I get enough clarity about the situation.

Like I mentioned before, I activated the Dog card #18 to represent a third party, and here we see the Dog is right in front of Dan. In this chain of houses, starting from the Dog, we can see the Dog (the third party) was the reason that the Love of Carla and Dan ended (the Heart in the house of the Coffin), and there were a lot of negative influences (Snake). The Dog was an enemy of Carla's love relationship with Dan (28). This is all explained by the "Chain of Houses" (the flow of meanings through the houses and the cards placed in them), starting from the Dog.

Let's follow the Chain of Houses:

- The starting point is the Dog (because we want to find out more about the Dog).
- You look in which house the Dog landed: The Dog landed in the house of the Heart.
- Now you look where the Heart card landed: The Heart card landed in the house of the Coffin.
- Now you look where the Coffin card landed: The Coffin card landed in the house of the Snake.
- Now you look where the Snake card landed: The Snake card landed in the house of the Dog.
- Now you look where the Dog card landed: The Dog card landed in the house of the Heart, and we arrived where we started the chain of houses.

Chain of houses starting from the Dog card #18

THE LENORMAND

1 Rider	2 Clover	3 Ship	4 House	5 Tree	6 Clouds	7 Snake	8 Coffin
9 Bouquet	10 Scythe	11 Whip	12 Birds	13 Child	14 Fox	15 Bear	16 Star
17 Stork	18 Dog	19 Tower	20 Garden	21 Mountain	22 Crossroad	23 Mice	24 Heart
25 Ring	26 Book	27 Letter	28 Man	29 Woman	30 Lily	31 Sun	32 Moon
		33 Key	34 Fish	35 Anchor	36 Cross		

Chain of houses starting from the Dog card #18

KNIGHTING TECHNIQUE

For the next step, I used the Knighting technique, starting from the Dog.

Starting from the left side of the Dog card: Move 2 cards to the left and then jump 1 up and 1 down. We get the Child card and the Rider card. This Child + Rider combination tells me a new love interest is coming in for Dan. Especially having the Rider in the house of the Lilies tells me it's somebody new in one's love life. Whenever it's about a love context and sex, the Lilies card shows up in my readings.

The Child card landed in the house of the Fox, and the Fox card landed in Dan's house (#28). This made me think that Dan started to do something wrong.

Now, we can Knight one more round starting from the Top of the Dog. So, we move two cards up, and then we jump to the left. We get the Coffin card, which indicates that this new love interest won't last long.

NOTE:

We cannot jump to the right because there are no more cards, and we cannot Knight from the Dog starting from the bottom of the Dog because there are no cards.

Three months later, I received feedback from Carla that her boyfriend Dan had met a new love interest, but it didn't last.

Knighting technique starting from the Dog card

Knighting technique starting from the Dog card

Having the Stork card right in front of Dan (28) showed me there will be an immediate change coming for him. What kind of change? The Dog is on top of the Stork, so I knew this new love interest would bring these changes. Also, the Dog is mirroring with the Ship card, which landed in the house of the Stork. That is another indication that the Dog brings changes. Having the Stork card in the house of the Moon, I knew it had to do with romance. In this picture, you see that the Dog card is mirroring to the Ship card on the other side of the Grand Tableau.

The Dog card is mirroring the Ship card

Now, don't forget Carla's question was all love-related, so every single card in the Grand Tableau is associated with Carla's love question. We are not looking to answer questions about work or health. The only health-related aspect in this Grand Tableau is that Dan (card # 28) has the Tree card very close located over his head, and the Tree card landed in the house of the Mice, and the Mice card landed in the house of the Book. This chain showed me that Dan would be very stressed and anxious if Carla discovered his secret.

Carla's feedback was that Dan did try to hide his secret from Carla. But in the end, she found out, and Dan was extremely stressed and anxious about this situation.

When we do the Knighting technique starting from the card #28 (Dan): We start at the top and move 2 cards up, then jump 1 to the left and 1 to the right. We get Child + Fish. Then we Knight from Dan's left side: we move 2 cards to the left, 1 up, and 1 down. We get House + Moon.

These card combinations from the Knighting technique tell me Dan will have a new (Child) romance (Moon) at his home (House) with lots of emotions (Fish).

Knighting technique starting from the Man card #28 (Dan)

THE LAST 4 CARDS IN CARLA'S GRAND TABLEAU

While I was shuffling the cards, I told my deck that the last 4 cards would be the outcome line for Carla's two relationships.

We have: Letter + Birds + Moon + Ring

These are all good cards that show there will be a lot of productive (Moon) communications (Letter + Birds) regarding the relationship (Ring).

When I looked at the last 4 cards, I knew everything would be fine in the end with Carla's relationships.

Carla's feedback after 3 months:

Carla's husband Paul found out about her relationship with Dan, and Carla discovered the secret that her boyfriend Dan tried to hide. She went through a very rough time, but in the end, she communicated extensively with her husband, Paul, and her boyfriend, Dan. The end of the story is that Carla and her husband stay together, and she breaks up with her boyfriend Dan on good terms, and they remain in contact as friends.

Remember, not every single card needs to be read in a Grand Tableau, and the context, the question, and the card combinations are extremely important to make an accurate prediction!

Chapter Forty-Five
Clearing the Cards

Before you do a card reading, you should clear your cards because the cards absorb the energies from previous readings, and you don't want the energies from your previous reading to influence the next one.

How to Clear the Cards

To clear the cards, you can smudge them one by one by burning white sage or palo santo wood. The smoke will banish any negativity. After smudging the cards, I put a black tourmaline crystal on top of the deck and leave it there until the next reading. A black tourmaline will protect and remove unwanted energies, returning the card deck to its neutral state.

Chapter Forty-Six
Conclusion

Congratulations on finishing reading my book! Thank you for keeping the Lenormand tradition alive!

In order to become an accurate Lenormand card reader, you need to practice daily and reread this book. You can practice with daily draws: just pull 3 to 5 cards for yourself every morning. You can ask, "What is awaiting me today?" or "What may I experience today?" By the end of the day, you will see how the cards you drew in the morning played out during your day. In time, you will understand how the cards talk to you. Make notes and keep journaling. You can also perform card readings for your friends and family and get feedback.

Wishing you the best of luck in your Lenormand journey!

Sylvia Ka'uhane

sylviakauhane@gmail.com